MYSTERIES *of* BLACKBERRY VALLEY

A Likely Story

ROSEANNA M. WHITE

Guideposts

A Gift from Guideposts

Thank you for your purchase! We want to express our gratitude for your support with a special gift just for you.

Dive into *Spirit Lifters*, a complimentary e-book that will fortify your faith, offering solace during challenging moments. Its 31 carefully selected scripture verses will soothe and uplift your soul.

Please use the QR code or go to **guideposts.org/ spiritlifters** to download.

Mysteries of Blackberry Valley is a trademark of Guideposts.

Published by Guideposts
100 Reserve Road, Suite E200
Danbury, CT 06810
Guideposts.org

Copyright © 2025 by Guideposts. All rights reserved. This book, or parts thereof, may not be reproduced, stored in a retrieval system, or transmitted in any form or by any means, electronic, mechanical, photocopying, recording, or otherwise, without the written permission of the publisher.

This is a work of fiction. Apart from actual historical people and events that may figure into the fiction narrative, all other names, characters, businesses, and events are the creation of the author's imagination and any resemblance to actual persons, living or dead, or events is coincidental. Every attempt has been made to credit the sources of copyrighted material used in this book. If any such acknowledgment has been inadvertently omitted or miscredited, receipt of such information would be appreciated.

Scripture references are from the following sources: *The Holy Bible, King James Version* (KJV). *The Holy Bible, New International Version* (NIV). Copyright © 1973, 1978, 1984, 2011 by Biblica, Inc. Used by permission of Zondervan. All rights reserved worldwide. www.zondervan.com.

Cover and interior design by Müllerhaus
Cover illustration by Bob Kayganich at Illustration Online LLC.
Typeset by Aptara, Inc.

ISBN 978-1-961442-62-7 (hardcover)
ISBN 978-1-961442-63-4 (softcover)
ISBN 978-1-961442-64-1 (epub)

Printed and bound in the United States of America
10 9 8 7 6 5 4 3 2 1

A Likely Story

Chapter One

Hannah Prentiss pushed through the swinging doors separating the kitchen from the restaurant floor, a tray of food in her hands for table twelve. The dinner rush was just getting started. Her server, Raquel Holden, had called in sick, so Hannah had happily set aside her orders and spreadsheets to cover for Raquel.

One of her favorite parts of running the restaurant was moments like this. Moments when she got to interact with crowds of hungry neighbors. When she saw the expressions of appreciation as they took their first bites, or watched them debate over the menu offerings, unable to decide which dish tempted them most today.

She slid plates of burgers and hand-cut chips onto the table in front of Alice Tyler and her twentysomething granddaughter, Jules, with a smile. "Here you go, ladies. Can I get you anything else?"

Before the Tylers could answer, the main door swung open. Ordinarily that wouldn't have stolen anyone's attention in the bustling restaurant, but Neil Minyard didn't just come in with the breeze. He charged inside like a force of nature, holding up a cardboard box as if it contained the secrets of the universe. "The books are here!"

Normally, that wouldn't have caused much of a ruckus either. No one else in town was ever quite as excited about books as Hannah's best friend's husband. Neil regularly went incommunicado when he got lost in the pages of a book in his favorite chair at his bookstore, Legend & Key.

This time, however, he might as well have been dressed as Santa in a room full of preschoolers. Shouts of enthusiasm arose, and the locals all jumped up to follow Neil through the dining room to an empty table at the back. Hannah wondered if tonight's packed crowd had as much to do with Neil as with the Hot Spot's new autumn menu items. Had he told everyone to come there for their book deliveries, rather than to his own shop?

Alice patted Jules's hand. "Go get ours, will you, sweet pea?"

Hannah settled a hand on Jules's shoulder, keeping her in her seat. "I'll bring it over. I have to get mine anyway. One or two?"

"Just the one," Alice said. "We'll share it. Sounds like this B.B. Smith fellow is already raking it in. He doesn't need that much of our help."

Hannah figured Alice was right about that. She had no idea how many sales *Blackberry Secrets* had acquired yet—only that it was enjoying its second week near the top of several national bestseller lists. She had no way of knowing what that meant for the author, whoever he or she might be.

Moving toward the line of locals who had swarmed Neil, Hannah took a spot at the back, near a table of unfamiliar faces. The diners must have found her restaurant from the highway or online, because they were frowning in clear confusion.

"Are we missing something?" asked a lovely gray-haired woman, who craned around Hannah to try to see what was going on.

Neil brandished a box cutter as if it were a legendary sword and attacked the packing tape.

Hannah chuckled at his antics. "A historical novel came out a couple weeks ago and has hit the bestseller lists—and it's set right here in Blackberry Valley, apparently. Neil, the bookstore owner acting like that tape is a monster putting up a fight, gave us all a discount for putting in a bulk order."

The woman's companion, a man who looked enough like her that he must be her brother, wore an expression of epiphany. "*Blackberry Secrets*? No kidding. I just downloaded the e-book. Haven't read it yet though. I knew it was set somewhere in the South, but didn't realize we'd stopped in the exact location. That's a fun coincidence."

"We're all pretty excited to read it." Hannah, her empty tray tucked under her arm, watched as Neil pulled fresh paperback copies out of the box. "Though I didn't realize he'd be hand-delivering them here." She supposed it made sense for him to bring a box to the Hot Spot, where quite a few of their mutual patrons would be gathered at this time of day. She certainly didn't mind, as it saved her a trip to the bookstore.

Two of her Wednesday regulars, Jim and John Comstock—identical twins in their fifties who styled themselves so differently that no one had any trouble telling them apart—were at the front of the line and took the first two copies from Neil's hands.

Hannah pressed her lips together, waiting for their commentary. She didn't know what form it would take, but those two always had something to say.

John scoffed loudly. "This cover's atrocious. If that's an actual photo from anywhere in Blackberry Valley, then I'm a swimsuit model."

A ripple of laughter rang out at the idea.

Jim, of course, couldn't be seen agreeing in public with his brother. "Oh, don't be such a snob. Book covers don't have to be perfectly accurate. They take artistic license to enhance the appeal. Personally, I like it. Nice colors, excellent contrast, and a good amount of drama. And I love this font. I think I have this one. It's called—"

"Nobody cares about the name of the font," John interrupted. But he was grinning. "Only you try to identify every font you see on every cover or billboard or menu."

Jim shot a smile over the crowd between them, straight at Hannah. "Nice use of both serif and sans serif on your menus, by the way. Perfect pairing."

Hannah smiled. "Thanks. I hired this great local graphics designer to help me."

Jim winked and flipped the book over to read the back cover. He'd all but begged her to let him do her menu design, claiming that if she hired it out to a bigger firm, he'd boycott the Hot Spot out of principle. Hannah hadn't been too worried about the threat, but since she was devoted to local small businesses as a farm-to-table restaurant, it only made sense to conform to that standard when having her menu designed.

Neil had his tablet out and tapped away at it between handing out books. The line moved quickly, though the neighbors lingered with their books rather than returning to their seats. Hannah didn't mind, even if it meant she had to nudge the fire chief, Liam Berthold, out of the way as she reached Neil.

Liam shot her a warm smile and granted her only a couple inches. To be fair, it was all the space he could make without bowling over Pastor Bob. "Now, now," he teased. "No need to get pushy.

There are enough books for everyone. Can I have your phone real quick?"

Knowing he was about to change his contact info again, as he often did when he saw her, she handed it over.

He tapped quickly then handed it back.

"Ah, yes. 'The Obstacle.' Because you were in my way just now." She had to laugh at the inside joke they'd come to share.

"I try to keep it fresh and interesting," Liam said.

Neil looked up, smiling when he saw her. "Hey, Hannah. Didn't think you'd mind if I did some delivering here. Jim mentioned when I saw him earlier that they'd be here for dinner, and it occurred to me that a lot of my other customers would be as well."

"Of course not." She hooked a thumb over her shoulder. "I told Alice I'd get hers too."

"Cool." He made a couple notes on his tablet and handed her two copies. "Lacy's coming in for dessert later. She said something about forgetting what you look like."

Hannah laughed and ran her fingers over the smooth matte finish of the book cover, loving the way the glossy embossed title felt in contrast. "It hasn't been *that* long. I saw her at church a few days ago."

"According to her, that doesn't count." He peered into the box, presumably counting the books left, cross-checked his list, and nodded. "She's worried you're overworking yourself. And she says your goat nieces and nephews will forget you if you don't come out for another visit soon."

Hannah had to laugh. She'd been meaning to make it out to her best friend's farm for a week. Or two. Time simply hadn't allowed it.

"She's one to talk. No one who gets up at four thirty in the morning gets to lecture anyone else about working too hard."

Neil grinned, hefting his box again. "She goes to bed early to make up for it though. Not your MO, from what I hear."

Given that the restaurant didn't stop service until ten, followed by cleanup and closing, he had a point. Rather than answer, she slid the tray onto the counter to be used again and waved the books as a farewell. "Thanks, Neil."

"Take the time to read it," he called after her as she wove her way back toward Alice. "It'll do you good."

She smiled. According to him, most problems could be solved with a good book and a few quiet hours. And it wasn't that Hannah disagreed, exactly. She loved a good novel as much as the next person. It was just that she spent so much time staring at her computer when she wasn't on the restaurant floor greeting customers, or supporting her chef in the kitchen, that the thought of opening a book made her eyes ache in protest some days. Not to mention that the busier the restaurant got, the less she could justify spending her free time reading for fun, as much as she would have loved more time to do so. It was a small price to pay for success, but one she felt keenly some days.

But she'd make an exception for *Blackberry Secrets*. After reading a few reviews in some of the social media groups she belonged to over the last week, she agreed it sounded like the sort of escape she would enjoy. A historical tale of a simpler time, full of mystery, suspense, and a touch of romance. And she was more than a little curious about how the author portrayed their little town.

Probably inaccurately. That was the usual complaint, right? Unless the author had spent a lot of time locally, they would get things wrong. And, according to town gossip, nobody knew anyone whose name could be shortened to B.B. Smith, the author's chosen moniker. Hannah prepped herself to forgive any errors. But as she handed Alice her copy with a smile, the pinch of the woman's lips made Hannah wonder if everyone else in town would do the same.

"Thanks." Alice took the book, frowning as she looked it over. "All that money for this? It's not even a hardcover."

"Neil gave us a great discount, Nan," Jules said. "I couldn't find it online for less. That's just what new books cost these days. Paper's expensive."

Alice harrumphed.

Jules chuckled. "Of course, if you'd let me get you an e-reader—"

"I don't need any more electronic doodads to figure out. I'd go back to my old flip phone if you'd let me. These smart ones just make me feel stupid."

"But you can adjust the size of the type on an e-reader. I think you'd like that, since you talk about how everyone prints their text too small these days."

"I like paper books." Alice set the book down and shot Hannah a glance that was surprisingly warm, given her complaints. "And I *am* looking forward to this one. I hope you enjoy it too, Hannah. I was thinking maybe we should have a book club to discuss it in a couple weeks, after everyone's read it. What do you think? Maybe here, so we can have refreshments. We could do it before you open. Evangeline won't let us have so much as coffee in her new meeting rooms in the library. Not that I blame her, with all the work that went into them."

"I'd love to have a book club here. If you end up organizing one, let me know the date and I'll reserve a few tables." Hannah smiled at each of the women and moved off.

Another order was up but it was for Dylan, the other server, so Hannah ducked into her office. The moment she stepped inside, the relative quiet wrapped around her. Rather than rush back out, she paused long enough to take a deep breath.

She ran her fingertips over the book cover again. Then she flipped through the pages. Not to read it yet, but to glance at the stylized chapter starts, see the pretty section dividers, and smile when familiar names jumped out at her.

Familiar roads. Familiar landmarks. Just a few seconds of flipping showed countless examples of those.

Then another familiar name caught her eye, and she halted the fan of her pages to see if her vision had deceived her.

Nope. Right there, on page 179. First line of the third paragraph.

Max knocked on the kitchen door of the Prentiss house, waiting for Hannah Jane to let him in. His gaze fell on the cookie jar, full as always. He wondered how many cookies were in it today. Hannah Jane would know down to the last crumb, and she looked at him as if he'd forgotten her warning about it from last time and might try to steal one.

They were probably dry and tasteless anyway.

Hannah blinked. It wasn't *her*—she knew that. Merely a fictional coincidence, no doubt. If the author had researched local names, Prentiss would have come up. And Hannah was a relatively common first name. Not to mention that her own middle name was Marie, not Jane.

Even so, she couldn't help the irrational surge of defensiveness. "My cookies are delicious, thank you very much." Then she had to laugh at herself.

With a shake of her head, Hannah set *Blackberry Secrets* on her desk and headed back out to the dining area. Everyone else in town might chatter about the book all evening, even before anyone had a chance to read it, but Hannah had work to do—people to feed, food to order, and a best friend to placate. She didn't have time to pore over more pages and figure out what role her name played in that story.

Even so, with her curiosity piqued, it promised to be a long, long night. And for once, she didn't intend to let a little thing like exhaustion keep her from reading before she went to bed.

Chapter Two

Thursdays were the middle of Hannah's work week, and sometimes that called for a pick-me-up. That, she told herself, was why she was striding into Jump Start Coffee for a latte and a pastry this morning, instead of pouring herself a cup from her own pot and sitting down with a bowl of cereal.

She glanced at her watch as she blustered in with the wind—the sun was still hot, but there was the slightest hint of cool to the breeze this morning, promising a break from summer's heat even if only by a few degrees. September didn't tend to bring truly brisk temperatures, but a little cooler would be nice.

She had to keep her visit here short. Invoices had somehow piled up again, and she couldn't let them go another day without attention. Plus they were expecting a shipment of produce from King Farm, family-owned and operated by Hot Spot hostess Elaine Wilby, and Hannah needed to be at the restaurant to receive and sign for it.

She'd hoped to have time to make it out to Lacy's farm, but it seemed unlikely to work out today. Maybe on Monday, when the restaurant was closed. She *did* want to visit the goats and hens—not to mention her best friend—but it seemed like these last couple of weeks, there was always something demanding her attention.

"Morning, Hannah." Jack Delaney picked up a carrier of lidded to-go cups. Rather nice of the newspaper's editor-in-chief to be the one to take coffee to his employees. He had a white bag in his hand too, no doubt filled with pastries.

"Morning, Jack. How's it going?"

"Not bad." He nodded to one of the four-top tables, around which several women from church were clustered. "I've been informed that this new book is big news, and I ought to be covering it."

Hannah's brows lifted, even as the women chuckled, one of them brandishing a copy of *Blackberry Secrets*.

"I'm telling you, Jack, this author is a local! You ought to do a big exposé," called Connie Sanchez, Grace Community Church's secretary.

Jack grinned on his way to the door. "Right. Tell you what, Connie—you figure out which of our neighbors is secretly a best-selling novelist, and I'll run the story."

"Deal!"

Hannah reached behind her to hold the door for Jack then resumed her place in line. Her position put her right beside the women's table. "What makes you all so sure B.B. Smith is really a local?"

The four ladies gaped at her with matching expressions of disbelief. "Are you serious?" asked Vera Bowman, a member of the church's women's group.

"Haven't you read the book yet?" Miriam Spencer, another women's group member, squinted at her, as if Hannah's question was the strangest thing she'd ever heard.

Hannah tilted her head. Neil had only delivered the books the night before. These women couldn't be finished already, could they? "I started it. I'm maybe five chapters in." What she'd read thus far had been good, but there hadn't yet been anything to make her certain that the author was one of her neighbors.

Connie tapped a finger on the cover. "This thing is too full of little tidbits no mere visitor could possibly know. Local nicknames for places, stories I don't know how anyone outside of town could have heard, and especially the people."

"The people?" Hannah inched forward a bit when the line shifted.

Miriam gave a decisive nod. "The characters in this book are not just characters. They're the real families and people who lived here in the 1930s."

"Really?" Hannah tried to recall the characters she'd been introduced to so far, but—other than her own, of course—she couldn't pull most of their names from memory. "You know, now that you mention it, I saw a Hannah Jane Prentiss mentioned when I was flipping through."

Miriam pointed a finger at her. "Your great-grandmother. You were named after her, you know."

She *did* know, though she hadn't paused to think about that when she'd seen the name. "So you're telling me that the character is the *real* Hannah Jane Prentiss? That my great-grandmother really counted the cookies in the jar?" It sounded ludicrous until she dug back in her memory, to the few recollections she had of her great-grandmother and the stories she remembered Grandpa telling about his mother. "You know, that actually makes sense. Grandpa loves to tell stories about how frugal she was. She apparently took 'waste not, want not' to whole new levels after living through the Great Depression."

Miriam chuckled. "She lived to be nearly ninety. I remember her pretty well. She ran the church's food pantry when I was young and kept inventory like nobody's business. Always knew the minute we were running low on something and put out the call for more."

Smiling, Hannah shifted forward with the line again. "That sounds about right."

Connie raised an eyebrow at Hannah. "Well, fair warning, sweetheart. It's not the spin this B.B. Smith puts on it. She comes off like a miser in here, and she isn't the only one who looks bad. This author smears the good names of half the families in Blackberry Valley. Paints them all as suspects in this theft and murder the hero's trying to solve."

Only one person stood between Hannah and the counter now, a woman she vaguely recognized as a customer but whose name she couldn't recall. Something that started with a *C* or a *K*, maybe. Hannah returned her attention to the women at the table. "Well it's just a novel. Fiction. Someone probably looked up census records or something and used real names of residents, but fictionalized their personalities."

"But they *didn't* fictionalize their personalities," Miriam contradicted. "That's the thing. They emphasized aspects in a more unflattering light than we like to remember, but they certainly didn't make it up altogether. Which makes a body wonder, doesn't it? What *else* does this author know about?"

Connie touched Miriam's arm, her eyes wide. "Shh! She hasn't read past chapter five yet. Don't spoil the book for her."

Miriam laughed, and Hannah did too, making a show of stepping away. "That's right, no spoilers, please." She lifted a hand. "I'll talk to you ladies later."

The woman ahead of her paid for her order. Zane Forrest, the owner of Jump Start Coffee, handed over a cinnamon bun saying, "There you go, Claire. I'll have your mocha out in just a minute. Hannah, you want your regular? I'll make it at the same time."

Claire, that was it. Claire Hanes. Hannah moved her smile from the woman to Zane. "Yep. Thanks, Zane."

While he went off to the espresso machine, Hannah looked at Claire again. "Morning, Claire. How are you today?"

"Basking in free time for the first time in months." Claire smiled and tucked a lock of dark hair behind her ear. "I miss the kids when they go back to school, but I'll admit it's nice to be able to take a deep breath."

Hannah chuckled, an image filling her mind of Claire and her husband and their two kids. They'd come in for dinner about a week ago to celebrate her daughter's birthday. She'd turned twelve, if Hannah recalled correctly. "I bet. I remember my mom feeling much the same about the start of school when my brother and I were young. And I don't remember our summers being nearly so busy with camps and activities as they are now. I don't think my sister-in-law comes up for air from Memorial Day to Labor Day." Hannah's brother, Andrew, had three children between the ages of five and nine with his wife, Allison.

"Tell me about it." Still grinning, Claire shook her head and tossed a glance over her shoulder at the table of women. "I keep seeing this book all over town. Maybe now I'll actually have time to read it. Do you know if Neil has it in stock at Legend & Key?"

"I know he got a bunch in for people who ordered them. I'll bet he ordered extra for those who missed out."

"Maybe I'll go check before I head home." When Zane returned to the counter with their coffees in hand, Claire took hers and then saluted him and Hannah with it. "Thanks. Good talking to you, Hannah. See you around."

"Enjoy your newfound freedom." Hannah took her coffee and then pointed to the pastries in the glass case. "Can I also get an apple fritter, Zane?"

"I insist. 'Tis the season, after all." Zane pulled one out with metal tongs and slid it into a paper bag. "The apples are fresh from the McIntyre orchard. I went out last weekend and picked them myself."

"Jacob told me." She grinned. "He's been experimenting with apple dishes all week." Jacob, the Hot Spot's head chef and Zane's older brother, planned to try a few more that morning, and then they'd make their final selections for the September menu. Her mouth watered at the memory of some of the things he'd already had her taste—apple pork chops, apple fritter bread, a savory tart with roasted apples, shallots, and bleu cheese.

"Tell him he should come up with a spin on Gram's baked apples as a side dish," Zane said as he rang up her purchase. "I woke up thinking about those this morning. She did something with them that I've never been able to replicate, but maybe Jacob will have better luck."

"I'll pass that along." She checked her watch again, debating whether she had time to sit and eat at the coffee shop. No, she'd better head back to the Hot Spot and enjoy her breakfast there. Saying goodbye to Zane and the women from church, she hurried out.

Once at the restaurant, she took a seat at her desk. Her invoices and spreadsheets still waited, but instead of dealing with those right away, she pulled forward her copy of *Blackberry Secrets*. She could read another chapter while she ate, then get down to business. She'd need Zane's hearty brew to kick-start her brain anyway.

As she read, she found it to be a different experience than it had been before her conversation with the women. She had initially approached it as a story that could have some hometown fun in it, if the author had done their research well. Now, she found herself wondering whether the hero, Max, represented someone she knew. Or, more likely, the ancestor of someone familiar, since the story was set in 1936.

Taking a bite of her fritter, Hannah savored the way the glaze melted in her mouth and paired so perfectly with the cinnamon and apple pieces nestled in the tender dough. How she loved apple season. Not that she couldn't enjoy an apple fritter any time of year, but she hadn't seen them before at Zane's coffee shop. He must do them seasonally. Washing the bite down with a sip of her coffee, she flipped to the next page in the book.

Her brows drew together as she read the end of a paragraph. It was about the main character, Max, walking home from town, but Hannah had never heard the name of the road he was on. Sweet Hollow Road? Where was that? It sounded like where Jonas Road should be, just outside of town, heading south.

She slid her bookmark back into place and used her mouse to bring her computer to life, ignoring her pastry for a moment. Maybe everyone was worried over nothing. No local would do something as obvious as use the wrong name for a road that their main character supposedly lived on. And for that matter, any outsider with access to the internet could look up a map. She did so now, just to verify her memory.

Yep. She found the place the story referenced with little effort, a mile outside of town, by the old mill that was now an antique shop. Jonas Road.

Pretty rookie mistake, as far as she was concerned. And so easily avoided that she had to shake her head. It had taken all of ten seconds to find the information. She was surprised the women from church hadn't noted it. In fact, hadn't Connie lived on Jonas Road for a while, before she and Hal built their current house? Yet Connie was convinced this book was written by someone currently living in Blackberry Valley.

Was Hannah missing something? Curious, she typed *Sweet Hollow Road Blackberry Valley* into her search engine, not sure what she expected to find.

But the first hit made her brows lift again. It was a 1945 article from the local paper's archives. She clicked on the link, the headline immediately making her breath catch.

SWEET HOLLOW ROAD TO BE RENAMED AFTER FALLEN WAR HERO FRANCIS JONAS.

"I stand corrected," she muttered to the screen, skimming the article. Moreover, she was impressed. Because that was the kind of detail that *she* would have gotten wrong, and she'd been born and raised here. She'd never once heard anyone refer to Jonas Road as Sweet Hollow—though there were other locations in town that had names used in speech that weren't on the signs, like Old Farm Road, which was technically Maple Street but no local called it that.

However, someone casually viewing a map would have gotten it wrong in their historical tale set in the 1930s, unless they had an actual map that predated the name change in 1945. Such maps surely existed. Neil had a bunch of them in his shop, documenting all of Blackberry Valley's history. He was as passionate about maps as he was about books. Still, it wasn't as if she could discover who the author was simply by asking Neil who had purchased—or looked at—maps dated before 1945.

But it wouldn't hurt to ask, would it?

After finishing the chapter and her breakfast, Hannah set the mystery aside to focus on her work. But later she might pay Neil a visit at Legend & Key, and see if this little detail could help her uncover author B.B. Smith's true identity.

Chapter Three

Blackberry Valley
April 6, 1936

Annabeth Billings gave the glass of the grandfather clock one final polish, moving the door back and forth in the light from the window to make sure no streaks marred the surface. Satisfied, she closed it with a soft click, smiling when the quarter hour chimed. She hummed along with the abbreviated song, running her cloth down the wood of the clock's case.

This was the last item on her cleaning list at the Prentiss house every week, in part because the carving was so intricate that it took a ridiculous amount of time to get the dust from every crevice, but mostly because she loved the old thing. Ending her day by feasting her eyes on its beauty left her in a good mood.

Once she'd finished, she stepped back to survey the gleaming wood, giving it a nod of approval. Then she scanned the rest of the room as she knew Hannah Jane would do soon, looking for anything out of place, any smudge unwiped, any speck of dirt on the floor. To her eye—arguably more trained than Hannah Jane Prentiss's, though the woman would never admit it—it was perfect. Certainly fit for the family gathering she knew would be held here in two days to celebrate Mr. Prentiss's birthday.

Idly, she wondered what kind of cake the woman would make for her husband. Annabeth had caught sight of a few of Hannah's creations in the last two years since she'd started cleaning for the Prentisses, and they were always gorgeous. Not, of course, that Annabeth had ever been offered so much as a leftover crumb. She was hired help—not family, friend, or neighbor, despite the fact that her house was only a mile away as the crow flew.

Proximity, as Reverend Cassidy had said last week, didn't make one a neighbor. Love did. In an ironic twist, which was surely not what the good reverend meant in his sermon on the parable of the Good Samaritan, that was why she had plenty of people who lived nearby, but few who considered her a neighbor.

To most of the people of Blackberry Valley, Annabeth Billings was from the wrong side of the proverbial tracks, born to a woman no one knew and even fewer people had ever learned how to talk to, and to a man they all looked at askance because of his oddities.

Her chest tightened at the thought of her parents. Sometimes, she still found herself wanting to sign her words along with speaking them, even though Mother had been gone for five years. And with Daddy only going to join her in heaven six months ago, Annabeth still expected to hear his greeting every time she opened the door to their small house.

They'd been good people. Misunderstood, but *good*. Daddy hadn't been able to help the deformities he'd been born with, the sight of which made people uncomfortable. Mother certainly hadn't been able to help that she'd gone deaf at age four after a bad fever.

Annabeth's fingers curled around her cleaning cloth. All she'd ever wanted to achieve in life was to help their neighbors understand them. And she thought she'd figured out how to do it. But she'd been too late. Too slow to learn. Too lacking in talent or skill or connections, or whatever it would have taken to see her words printed in something that others would read.

Words could change the world, Daddy had always said. Stories could open people's hearts and eyes.

She believed that—but no one except Sammy had ever read hers. Well, and Miss Markwood, who'd been the only teacher to ever tell her she could amount to something someday.

She was still waiting on someday. At the moment, she had nothing to show for her twenty-three years but a series of houses she polished to a shine once a week then had to polish again the next. Nothing but calluses on her hands and cupboards always bordering on too empty. A house that could fit entirely in this one room of the Prentiss home, and whose repairs she didn't know how she'd manage now that Daddy was gone.

But that dim future didn't bear thinking about right now. Right now, she could push that aside and be grateful that winter was over, that she had jobs enough to keep *something* on her table, and that Sammy had invited her to spend Saturday evening helping her watch her younger brothers and sisters while their parents were out. She loved those evenings spent at the Adams house. It was a promise that would get her through the week.

Making her way to the kitchen, Annabeth fully expected Hannah Jane Prentiss to be stationed at the stove this time of day. But, though three different pots simmered, sending up a heavenly cloud of aromas that made her stomach growl, the mistress of the house was nowhere in sight. After stowing the Murphy's Oil Soap that she used for polishing back under the sink where it belonged, Annabeth peeked into the pantry then out the door at the porch. There was still no sign of Hannah Jane, so she resigned herself to waiting.

This was the one room of the house that she was never asked to clean, other than washing the windows and scrubbing the baseboards every few months. It was less familiar to her than the rest of the house, so she let her gaze wander over the cabinets, the old table, the pretty glass cookie jar with its just-as-pretty cookies inside, like something from a Norman Rockwell illustration.

"I've counted those cookies, Annie Billings. I'll know if you took one."

Having expected it, Annabeth didn't jump at the voice coming from the hallway—the woman must have been in the powder room. She turned to face one of her many employers with a bright smile. "It would be easier if you weighed the jar before and after I was here. That would account for any crumbling."

Though only three years her elder, Hannah Jane had no trouble at all with the stern expression that no doubt kept her toddler in line. "My cookies don't crumble."

Annabeth kept her grin in place. "Which I would know if I'd ever taken one, and you know well I haven't." She motioned toward the sink. "Cleaning supplies have been put away and everything done. Is there anything else you need me to do today, Mrs. Prentiss?"

She could never make herself call Hannah Jane *Mrs. Prentiss* in her thoughts—how could she, when she remembered her from school? But aloud, she kept to the manners expected of someone in her position.

Hannah Jane first checked under the sink to make certain the polish was really back in its place—as if

Annabeth might make off with it for some reason—then spun around and clicked through the house on her pumps, her apron still tied over her pristine blue dress. As if she expected Mr. Rockwell to drop by any moment and paint her for the cover of the *Saturday Evening Post*, with a caption of "The Perfect Housewife."

Holding her spot in the kitchen, Annabeth curled her fingers into her palm, the bite of nails in skin meant to remind her to be more charitable. *She's trying to make a good home for her family*, Mother would have reminded her. *And she tries to control what she can because of what she can't. You know she lost both her siblings in that car crash.*

Leave it to Mother to correct every snippy thought, even years after she'd passed away. To make her see everyone in a softer light, despite them never showing that same softness toward anyone in the Billings family.

Hannah Jane reentered the kitchen, her nod the closest thing to approval she ever gave. Well, along with the money she counted out from her purse, and the words that guaranteed Annabeth would be able to keep on scraping by. "I'll see you next Tuesday."

"I look forward to it, Mrs. Prentiss. I hope your husband's birthday celebration is wonderful."

The woman didn't even smile at the mention of it. If anything, her lips pressed tighter. "Be sure the door latches properly on your way out. It's been sticking."

"I will." Annabeth let herself out the kitchen door, pulling the main door firmly shut and pushing the contrary screen back into place too, with extra care.

Though she cast a glance toward town, she didn't let her feet carry her in that direction. Given the hollow rumbling of her stomach, she'd be too tempted to spend some of the money in her pocket on a hot meal at the diner.

She headed for home instead, turning from Main Street onto Sweet Hollow Road and trying to remember what she had in her cupboards. She hadn't thought to get any beans soaking last night, but she had some eggs from that morning, and there was still flour. She could make some noodles and use the chicken broth she'd made the other day from the bones Sammy had given her. There'd even been a few scraps of meat left on them, which would go nicely with the noodles. Did she still have any carrots or celery? She couldn't remember, but if so, that would make a fine soup. And the noodles wouldn't take long to cook. Well, once she got them rolled out and cut up.

Maybe she'd just make drop dumplings instead. Same idea, but quicker.

Twenty minutes later, she'd let herself into the little cabin that had always been home and started her dinner. She tidied up while it simmered, humming one of Daddy's favorite hymns, but her mind had already wandered from chores and even the promise of food. It had gone back to the stack of paper sitting on the thirdhand desk and the sheet still in the secondhand typewriter—a gift from Sammy four Christmases ago and without question the most precious thing she could claim as a possession.

As a matter of discipline, she didn't let herself sit down at the desk until after she'd eaten and cleaned up. But then, at what felt like long last, she carried her oil lamp over—this old cabin had not been wired for electricity like the houses in town—and settled onto the faded cushion she'd made for the chair. She reread the paragraphs she'd left finished the previous night.

Max Stuart knew better than to accept Tom Dawson at his word. He'd heard the man lie through his teeth more times than he'd heard the cows lowing in George's pasture. Dawson knew more than he was letting on. Max would have staked his new hat on it, had he been a man prone to wager.

Of course, there was nothing to do but smile. "Good to know, Tom. Thanks." Max waited until the man strode away and then pulled out his notebook, writing down not just what the man had said, but what he hadn't. The way his finger had twitched when he claimed he hadn't seen Elmira since church on Sunday, the way his eyes had darted to and fro.

There was something there. But something helpful to the question? That was yet to be determined.

Annabeth tapped her fingers on the keys, sifting through her mind for the next sentence she'd mentally written while she worked today. She knew that her Elmira character would be the victim of this murder mystery, but she hadn't sorted out yet what led to the tragedy—this small side mystery her hero, Max, was working on would lead into the main story and the discovery of the body.

She just had no idea why someone had killed her fictitious schoolmarm, nor what had led the respectable young woman to go out alone at night. But Annabeth would sort all that out. Discovery was part of the fun of writing.

Now, who would be the one to find the missing schoolmarm in the ditch? She'd been toying with a few different options, but she had a good idea of what would work best. Which meant she'd better introduce the character.

Her lips twitching into another smile, Annabeth settled her fingers on the keys and started typing.

After consulting his list, Max turned onto Main and made his way to the Prentiss house at the edge of town. Hannah Jane Prentiss had made it clear she didn't care for him, but she tolerated him the way one tolerated the cold in winter—with a stiff upper lip but no affection. He knew better than to knock on her front door, where she'd take one look at him and close the door in his face, but he didn't mind going to the kitchen door instead. That was where she'd be this time of day.

Sure enough, she opened the door to him with a bit of a scowl, but she invited him into the kitchen.

"Afternoon, Mrs. Prentiss," he said. "Just stopped by for the mending you have for my mother."

"Of course. Let me go fetch it." She paused on the threshold of the door to the rest of the house, frowning at him over her shoulder. "And I've counted the cookies in the jar, Maxwell Stuart. I'll know if you sneak one."

Annabeth chuckled as she typed it out. She knew she'd have to change the names of all her neighbors if she ever meant to get this novel published. But for now, her father's name was the only one she'd changed. Matthew Billings had become Maxwell Stuart. But

A Likely Story

everyone else—well, this was her way of working through the frustrations, getting them all out of her system so she could go on smiling at her neighbors.

She'd dropped them all into her mystery, and they'd soon be suspects in the imaginary murder of her fictitious schoolmarm. And it would be Max who solved it all, who saved the day and a few more lives besides. Max who brought the justice to her made-up world that no one had ever shown her father in reality.

Maybe it was too late to change her neighbors' understanding of her parents in this life with her writing. But there would still be poetic justice in showing, through her characters, what a hero Daddy had been and what a beautiful soul Mother was—not that Max had met his future wife yet. That would happen in the next chapter.

A dash of reality. A whole lot of imagination in the plot. And hopefully, a story someone would actually want to read someday.

If Annabeth ever got up the nerve to send it off to a publisher.

Chapter Four

Hannah strode into Blackberry Valley Library and aimed herself at the front desk. She'd received an email that morning saying her interlibrary loan request had come in, so she'd carved out a few minutes on this Friday afternoon to stop in and grab it.

Head librarian Evangeline Cooke greeted her with a smile and pulled out the cookbook Hannah had requested, part of its cover obscured by a cardstock sleeve with the loan details on it. "Here you go, Hannah."

"Thanks, Evangeline." Hannah tugged the book toward her and flipped through it.

Often she ended up buying the cookbooks she first requested through the library, but she liked to make certain they would prove useful first. This one was all about autumn recipes, and if the offerings were as good as they sounded from the table of contents she'd been able to view online, it seemed likely to become a permanent part of her collection. She and Jacob always scoured books, the internet, and their own imaginations for inspiration when developing the menus for each season.

She took a moment to appreciate the cover with its apples and pumpkins—or as much of it as she could see behind the loan sleeve—then flipped through a few pages. "Oh good," she said softly when she saw that each recipe had at least one photograph accompanying it, sometimes several. Jacob had an artist's eye and could make something beautiful with or without visual guidance, but she personally appreciated seeing the finished product of a recipe before she attempted to create it herself.

Her phone vibrated in her pocket, and she pulled it out to see a text from Elaine, asking when she'd return to the restaurant. Apparently the day's delivery from King Farm didn't match the order, and Jacob was asking how to handle it.

Rather than try to type out a long answer, she simply replied that she'd be back in a few minutes and abandoned any thought of further browsing in the library. Instead, she dug in her purse for her library card.

"This everything for you today?" Evangeline asked as she grabbed her scanner.

Hannah held out her card. "Sure is, thanks."

A burst of laughter from a table to the right drew her gaze, part of her expecting Evangeline or another librarian to hush the group. She didn't recognize any of the people at the table—three seniors and one woman who looked to be in her fifties—but they didn't seem to be cowed by the library's reputation for silence.

"Right, Jill," the youngest one was saying, sarcasm saturating her voice and coloring her smile. "There's a treasure buried outside of town. No question."

"Well, why not? Everything *else* in the book seems to be true," a white-haired man replied.

"Not *everything*," one of the older two women said. Jill, maybe? "No one's saying there was really a murder like in the story. But the author certainly seemed to draw on real local history for everything else. I'm just saying the part about buried money could be true too."

Someone from another table lobbed a "Shh!" at the noisy group, who obligingly reverted to whispers.

Hannah found herself wishing they hadn't. *"Blackberry Secrets?"* she asked Evangeline, who probably knew all about the book by this point.

The librarian smiled. "What else? It's been the hot topic in here all week. Have you read it yet?"

"I'm about halfway through." She certainly knew about the crime in the book, but she had yet to come across any mention of treasure. "There's something in there about buried money?"

"I won't spoil the book for you, but to keep it vague—yeah." Evangeline nodded toward the quartet. "They aren't the only ones who have been in here today speculating about how much truth is in that novel. Everyone's been digging through whatever we have in the historical collection that might tell them more about Blackberry Valley in 1936. I suspect they hope it will help them figure out where this supposed treasure might be buried."

"Seriously? Man, I need to finish this book." Hannah was beginning to feel very out of the loop. And if she didn't catch up quickly, she'd be the only person in town who *hadn't* figured out who the author was.

Evangeline chuckled and slid the cookbook over to her, a receipt with the due date nestled between two of the pages. "Hope you enjoy it—and this too."

"Thanks. Have a great day." Cookbook in hand, Hannah darted one last glance at the still-whispering foursome and made for the doors.

A bulletin board caught her eye on the way out. She stopped to study the collage of flyers and posters, not entirely sure what had snagged her attention at first. Then she realized that it was a flyer offering help with ancestry research—which was printed in the same font combination that the Hot Spot used on their menus.

That made sense when she saw that the ad's contact info was for John Comstock. No doubt Jim had designed it for him, and he must have had this font combo on his brain after doing their last menu updates.

She continued out to her car, the well-designed flyer lingering in her thoughts as she slid behind the wheel. When her phone rang a second later with a call from Lacy, she put it through to her hands-free and smiled. "Hey, Lacy."

"Have you figured out who this B.B. Smith person is yet?"

Hannah laughed as she backed out of her parking spot. "Why do you think *I* would have?"

"Because you're always figuring stuff out. I ran into town this morning for a few errands, and I must have heard the same conversation five times, all folks wondering who the author could be. I told them all it was you—obviously. You have nothing but time on your hands for things like novel-writing, after all."

Putting her car in gear, Hannah headed for the street. "Is that your subtle way of reminding me that I still haven't made it out to visit you?"

"Sprout misses you. You should see how big she's gotten."

The very thought of the baby goat she'd had the privilege of naming made Hannah consider turning toward Bluegrass Hollow Farm instead of the Hot Spot. If it wasn't for that text from Elaine, she might have given in to the temptation. "I'm so sorry. You know I *want* to come and hang out, but it seems like there's a new fire to put out every day. That's why I'm currently headed back to the restaurant, where a delivery was apparently wrong."

"You know I get it. Though you *also* know you need to take some time for yourself at some point. And if that time for you happened to involve me, I wouldn't complain."

"Neither would I. Well, I'll for sure see you at church on Sunday. And I'll come help with chores Monday morning, since apparently church doesn't count."

Lacy's laughter filled the car as Hannah eased to a stop behind a ridiculously long line of traffic. What was up with that? And the tags on the car in front of her were from Minnesota, of all places. "Hannah, helping with chores—appreciated as it always is—is not *relaxing*. And that's what you need. Time to unwind and unplug."

"Hey, I'm unplugged when I'm at your farm." She drummed her fingers on the steering wheel, suddenly wishing she'd walked to the library. What was the holdup? "And I like helping out, so it should count as unwinding."

Lacy's sigh blustered over the phone. "Pathetic. We're going to plan some *real* unwinding too. A girls' night or something. Where we go somewhere that's neither your place with your work nor my place with my work. Dinner and a movie maybe. Think of what would be fun."

"I will. Promise." Traffic finally started moving when a giant RV pulled off the road up ahead. Someone was climbing up the ladder on the back and onto the roof by the time she drove by. With a camera in hand. "What in the world?"

"What?" Lacy asked.

"There's a huge RV with Florida tags parked on the side of the road, with someone on the roof taking pictures."

Lacy laughed again. "Neil said the town's been flooded with tourists the last two days, eager to see the setting of their new favorite book. Have you noticed more tourists than usual at the Hot Spot?"

"Now that you mention it, there were more unfamiliar faces than familiar ones in the crowd last night." She sneaked one more glance at the RV photographer in her rearview mirror but otherwise kept her focus on the road ahead. "Have you finished the book yet? Tell me I'm not the only one who hasn't."

"I have five chapters to go," Lacy reported.

"I was just at the library, and people were talking about a treasure they think might be buried somewhere around town. Have you gotten to that part yet?"

"Sort of. It's been mentioned. I don't want to spoil anything for you. But are you serious? People think it's real?"

"They've argued that plenty of other things from the book are real."

"That's interesting."

Hannah turned at the intersection, her gaze homing in on the restaurant. "You know what else I saw at the library? A flyer saying John Comstock is available to help with ancestry research. I didn't know he did that sort of thing. Did you?"

"No. Though he *is* a history teacher, so I guess it shouldn't be too surprising that he'd be interested in family histories as well as general history. Does that have something to do with the novel?"

"I don't know." She hadn't actually thought it through, but it was niggling at her. "I didn't know John was interested in ancestry. And Jim knows more about the publishing industry than anyone else in town, given his design work. He's done book covers for some independent authors, hasn't he?"

"He has. Are you thinking one of the Comstock twins could be B.B. Smith?" Lacy asked.

"Or both of them, working together? Perhaps B.B. stands for Brother, Brother." It would lend some irony to the twins' commentary on the cover the other night, but it was exactly the sort of irony they'd enjoy. "I don't know. But it's the first thought I've had about who the author might be that makes any sense at all." She pulled into her usual parking spot. "And it's Friday, which means John and his wife will likely be in for an appetizer and soda while they're waiting to pick up their granddaughter from dance practice. Maybe I can fish a little."

"Well, if your fishing results in a nice catch, let me know. Hey, I have to run. My mom just got here."

"And I just pulled in at the restaurant. Talk to you later, Lacy. Tell your mom I said hi."

"I'm sure she says it back. Later, Hannah."

Hannah disconnected and shut off her car, grabbed the cookbook and her purse, and hurried into the kitchen entrance of the restaurant. She didn't see the King Farm delivery truck in the lot, so whatever the mistake was, they apparently weren't concerned about hanging around to figure it out.

"Hey," Jacob said as she bustled in, nodding toward the crates of vegetables. "They mixed up the numbers of butternut squash and cabbages. They had other deliveries to make, so they couldn't hang around. But they said they'd stop on their way out of town if we wanted to send the extra cabbage back with them."

Hannah surveyed the produce, hands on her hips. "The cabbage should keep fine. We just won't have to order as much next week. But we're going to need that butternut if the Better with Butternut Bisque keeps moving like it has been this week."

Jacob nodded. "I thought the same. Then I thought maybe you'd want us to feature the slaw we tested yesterday to try to move more cabbage and less soup."

It wasn't a bad idea, generally speaking. Though, apparently word of the soup had spread through town. They'd had quite a few people come in the last two days specifically to try it after hearing how good it was. "We can feature the new slaw as a special to encourage people to try it. But I think we're still going to need the squash." She flashed her chef a smile. "The hazard of such a great recipe on a seasonal menu. Everyone wants to try it before it goes away."

Jacob grinned and went back to his cutting board, where the last of the previous batch of butternut was waiting for his knife. "It did turn out rather well."

Elaine hustled into the kitchen with an apologetic smile. "Sorry about the mix-up. I told the delivery driver we'd sort it out."

Hannah waved away the apology. "No big deal. I'll text them and let them know they don't need to pick up the cabbage, but we could use the squash on their next trip to town."

Elaine nodded. "I can always bring the missing stuff with me tomorrow, if it'll fit in my car."

"It should. Thanks, Elaine." Hannah nodded toward the boxes. "Are you willing to help move it all into the walk-in?"

They finished the task in no time, and the hostess returned to her pre-opening tasks while Hannah put all the fruits and veggies in their proper places in the room-size refrigerator. By the time she'd finished, she was glad to step back into the warm kitchen and shake the chill off her fingers. She breathed in the rich scents of the food already underway and let out a happy sigh.

Then she checked her watch. "One hour until opening." Raquel and Dylan would arrive in the next twenty minutes to prep for their shifts.

The next hour sped by as they readied the restaurant, and as soon as they unlocked the doors, guests streamed inside. Hannah took special note of those she recognized and those she didn't. Neil was right about there being more travelers than usual, but could that really be because of a book that had only been a short time?

Introducing herself to several of the new people, Hannah asked where they were from and what had brought them to Blackberry Valley. Most of the visitors had made a point to stop in town as they were driving through the area for other reasons, to see the setting of the book.

She was covering the hostess station during Elaine's break when John Comstock and his wife, Gina, walked through the doors. They always came in after dropping their granddaughter off at her dance class, and nearly always chose either an appetizer or dessert to share while they waited. "Hello," she said as they entered, noting immediately that John looked far less cheerful than usual. "Are you two going to want an app this evening, or dessert?"

Gina sent her husband an encouraging smile and bumped his arm. "I always say sugar makes everything better."

John grinned down at her, but it didn't quite meet his eyes. "So do nachos."

"Cheese versus sugar—a debate that won't be solved in our lifetime, I'm sure." Hannah grabbed two menus and motioned for the couple to follow her. "Clearly the answer is to get an app *and* dessert tonight."

"I think you may be right," Gina agreed.

Hannah led them to one of Dylan's tables and slid the menus in front of them. She caught John's gaze. "Everything okay?"

He sighed and rubbed his eyes. "It's no big deal, really. Just frustrating. I decided to try to make a little extra money by starting an ancestry research business. Jim designed me some flyers to put up around town and post online."

"I saw one at the library." Hannah smiled. "Looked great."

He didn't cheer any at the compliment. "Yeah, well, it apparently wasn't great timing on my part, with everyone looking for this B.B. Smith guy all over town. Penny Barrett cornered me in the teacher's lounge today and accused me of being the author, saying my historical research skills made it obvious. Everyone at school had heard about it by the end of the day, and you'd think I'd come down with the plague. No one would listen when I said I haven't written fiction since *I* was in school, and nothing longer than an article in my entire life."

Hannah drew in a long breath. She'd had the same thought, hadn't she? Not that she would have lobbed it as an accusation or treated him like a pariah for it. "I don't get it. Even if you *were* the author, why would it make people treat you like that?"

Gina reached across the table to pat her husband's hand where it rested beside his napkin-wrapped flatware. "I guess you haven't finished the book yet."

She was going to have to remedy that soon. "Not yet."

"A lot of dirty laundry from several Blackberry Valley families got aired in that book—things people are none too keen on everyone knowing about their grands or great-grands."

Hannah frowned. "But all that's ancient history. It's from nearly a hundred years ago."

"Not so ancient, when you consider how touchy some people can be about family." Gina shook her head. "If that novel has as much truth in it as it seems, then our neighbors are the grandchildren of thieves, gossips, embezzlers, misers—"

"Well, it's not like anyone's ancestor is a murderer." John leaned against the back of the booth. "I'll admit that I was none too happy with whoever wrote that book when I saw how my grandmother was portrayed. But I have a bit more sympathy for whoever it is now. No wonder they're using a pen name."

Hannah glanced around the restaurant with its mix of familiar and unfamiliar faces, some laughing, some having serious conversations with their companions, some studying the menu. How many of the townspeople were upset by the book? And how many of the strangers were tourists, eager to see if the real-life residents of Blackberry Valley were like their fictional—or not-so-fictional—ancestors? "If people are reacting like that, then I have my doubts the author's ever going to come forward, assuming they really live here."

"Not voluntarily. But we'll figure out who it is." John's eyes were hard. "You can bet I'll be trying to. Nothing short of a signed confession from someone else is going to convince everyone at school it isn't me."

Hannah buttoned her lips against all her own reasoning. John was clearly upset by the allegation. His attitude could be a deflection, a clever misdirection, even genuine distress at being called out so quickly, covered up with a claim of innocence. In that case, Gina would obviously be in on it.

But he seemed earnest. At the very least, Hannah wasn't about to jump onto the accusation train. She offered the Comstocks a smile and tapped her finger on the table. "Dylan will be with you shortly. And know that we are always here for you with cheese and sugar, no matter what."

At least she left them laughing as she returned to the hostess stand.

Chapter Five

Hannah lifted her coffee cup to her lips, only then noticing it was still empty—just like it had been five minutes ago. Or ten? Twenty? Rather than check her watch or get up to refill her cup, she flipped another page in *Blackberry Secrets*.

She'd been snuggled up on her couch since the crack of dawn, novel in hand and a notebook at her side. She was actually glad she hadn't made it further into the book yet. It hadn't occurred to her at first to take notes while she read, but after her conversation with the Comstocks last night, she decided it would be wise.

Because clearly everyone in town was trying to figure out who the author was—and apparently many of them weren't exactly waiting with praise and accolades. At some point, as she worked last night then fell into an exhausted sleep, she'd decided that B.B. Smith would need a friend when their true identity came out, assuming the author really was a local.

Someone had clearly spent a lot of time on this book. The writing alone must have taken months or years, to say nothing of the research. The town of nearly a century before was painted with depth and life and beauty. The characters were all so multifaceted and *real* that she almost expected to see them walking along when she glanced out her window.

And while some of those facets were admittedly negative, she honestly didn't know why anyone was upset about them. Not a single character was *all* negative. Case in point—Hannah Jane Prentiss. Yes, she counted the cookies in her jar, but after she found a dead body, her character had experienced quite a lot of growth and change.

Was any of it true of her great-grandmother? Obviously she'd never found a murdered schoolmarm—that story would still be told in the family if there was even a whiff of truth to it.

But from what Hannah could remember of her great-grandmother, and from stories about her life, she had been similar to her fictional version by the end of the book. A caring mother. A devoted wife. Someone who would protect her family so fiercely that sometimes she didn't see others clearly, but who could admit when she was wrong and would stay loyal to a friend no matter what.

Even knowing the novel was just that—something an author had made up—Hannah still felt like she was getting to know her great-grandmother better through the story. Whoever B.B. Smith was, they'd uncovered something true about her family in their research, something that made her love that family all the more.

Because they were *real*. They were complicated. They were such a true-to-life mixture of counting every crumb yet giving generously, even when money was tight. *That* was the woman who had run the food pantry and made sure it was always stocked—the same one who saved every button and let not a single scrap of anything go to waste.

And her ancestor wasn't the only one the author treated so honestly. Each townsperson who had a negative trait also had a positive one. Some came off better than others, but no one was shown in black or white.

That was where her notes came in. She'd jotted down the names of every character and listed their flaws and virtues as presented in the story. Some tipped more heavily toward one column, some toward the other. The hero, Max Stuart, did a great job of viewing them fairly, even when he was treated badly by someone.

Picking up her pen, she jotted a couple more notes as Max delivered the line that finally named the culprit—a character with an unfamiliar surname that Hannah felt was as fictional as Max himself. She'd certainly never heard of anyone in town with either of those last names. And she intended to cross-check them both against online census records for the region, after she finished the story.

The last chapter flew by, leaving her with a smile on her face as she finished. She set the book on a cushion and stretched. Her stomach growled, and no wonder. A glance at her watch showed her that it was noon already. Hannah decided to eat lunch while she did that census research then get downstairs to prep the restaurant for their final open day this week. Saturdays were always busy.

Five minutes later, she sat at her computer with a sandwich beside her. It took some effort to resist the urge to open her email, but she knew if she gave in, she'd tumble down the rabbit hole of work and completely forget about this research she wanted to do. So she navigated to a search engine instead and looked up Kentucky census records. It took her a few minutes to find a site that would let her view results without paying for them—though she still had to create an account—but once there, it was a quick process to search for the names she didn't recognize from the book.

She'd been right. Neither of the last names appeared in records for the county at the time in question, which meant that both the hero and villain of the story were entirely fictional. At the very least, if they were based on real people, their names had been changed.

She took a bite of her turkey and cheddar with crisp, locally grown lettuce and pulled her notes in front of her, propping the notebook on her laptop's keyboard. If the book was written by a local, it stood to reason that their family either wasn't represented in the book at all or was cast in a favorable light, right? There was logic to it, anyway.

Finding the families in Blackberry Valley who were present at the time, but did not appear in the book, promised to take far more time than she had to give right now. She jotted the idea down but focused on the second half of her thought.

Who had the author portrayed most favorably in the story?

None of the families were perfect, but a few stood out. The Adamses, the Tylers, and a Reverend Cassidy.

Her brows knit. She knew a few Adamses. She didn't know anyone in town with the surname Cassidy, although it sounded familiar.

Tyler, though. She certainly knew the Tylers.

The thought of Alice having written the novel—what with her aversion to technology and her snarky comment about the author not needing her money—was absurd enough to make Hannah's lips twitch. Was the older woman that good an actress, that she could pretend to be put out at having to buy a book, and by its cost? She knew for a fact that Alice's sole computer was a dinosaur of a machine that she only kept to play card games on. Or so she'd said at a meeting of the church's women's group a few months before, when someone was asking for volunteers to make a flyer.

Alice surely wouldn't have lied about that. But was it even possible to submit a book for publication these days without the help of a computer?

So, Alice was unlikely to be the author, but someone in the Tyler family might be. Alice had two sons and quite a few adult grandkids. Like Jules, who worked in administration at a nearby community college.

Which meant Jules was educated, and certainly she was technology savvy, as evidenced by her continual effort to bring her grandmother into the twenty-first century. And she was an avid reader. Hannah had seen her at the library and Neil's store on several different occasions, always with a stack of popular novels in a variety of genres.

Too bad the question Hannah had texted Neil—asking whether anyone had bought pre-1945 maps of Blackberry Valley—was a dead end. It would have been handy to have a list of people to compare with this one.

Her sandwich finished, Hannah got up to put her plate in the kitchen sink then meandered to the window overlooking Main Street. Enjoying the stretch of her legs after sitting so long with the book, she stayed there for several minutes, watching a steady stream of pedestrians go by, many looking as though they were on a mission.

When she spotted Alice and Jules Tyler, she didn't pause to do more than grab her keys before dashing out to intercept them. She had no particular plan, but the coincidence of their strolling by so soon after she'd been thinking of them was too good to pass up. Locking her apartment door behind her, Hannah raced down to the street.

Once on the sidewalk, she released a breath of relief that Alice wasn't a power-walker. The two women were still visible, following in the path of a veritable stream of other locals all heading into city hall.

"Hey, Hannah. Going to the meeting?"

At Liam Berthold's voice, Hannah spun around, suddenly very aware that she still wore the comfortable elastic-waisted shorts and faded college T-shirt she'd been lounging in. She'd planned to change before she went down to work but hadn't gotten that far. But he smiled at her as if he didn't even notice what she was wearing—which could well be true. Guys were known for that, right?

Clearing her throat, she focused on his words instead of his possible reaction to her outfit. "Meeting?"

Liam motioned to the city hall building. "Wyatt Granger called an emergency meeting for any business owners and homeowners whose properties were mentioned in *Blackberry Secrets*, though it's open to anyone who wants to attend. I don't think the Hot Spot is on the list, but I thought maybe you were coming out of curiosity."

She shook her head. Now the town council was involved? "I hadn't heard about it. Not that I'm opposed to going, if it's open to the public."

"It is. And it looks like word has spread quickly, given the number of people going in." He led her forward with a brief touch to her elbow.

Hannah watched a handful of people hurry into the building, almost all of them wearing business attire. Her shorts and T-shirt felt way underdressed for this, but curiosity made her fall in beside Liam anyway.

"I just finished reading *Blackberry Secrets* this morning," she said. They trotted up the few steps to the front of the building. She could catch up with the Tylers afterward, if it still seemed important. "Did Wyatt say what this meeting is about specifically?"

"Nope." As they filed into the half-filled auditorium, Liam motioned to a row of still-open seats. "Want to sit together?"

"Sure." She followed him into the row and took a seat. She caught sight of her dad and Uncle Gordon on the other side of the room, a few rows down. They must be curiosity-seekers too. They didn't own a business mentioned in the book, and while there was a Prentiss house in the story, it was no longer in the family. Though the fact that Hannah Jane Prentiss had been in the novel was certainly enough to account for their interest.

Dad sent her a grin and a wave. He exchanged a few words with his brother then both of them stood up and came to join her and Liam.

"Hey there, sweetie." Dad moved in to claim the chair on her right, Uncle Gordon following him. "Glad you made it. You didn't answer my text."

"Text?" She reached for her pocket, only to realize she hadn't even grabbed her phone when she made her spontaneous dash down the stairs. "Whoops. Sorry, Dad. I've been unplugged all morning, reading *Blackberry Secrets*. I didn't even see you'd texted."

Dad waved away her apology. "No big deal. I was just letting you know we were coming to this and wondered if you wanted to join us, since the Prentiss family played such a role in the book. But here you are." He leaned around her to ask Liam, "Any idea what this is about, Chief?"

It stood to reason that if there was a real emergency, the fire chief would know about it. But again, Liam shook his head. "I'm as in the dark as the rest of you."

Before they could muse any further on what the meeting might be about, Wyatt Granger, town councilman and head of Blackberry Valley's business association, stepped up to the podium with a smile that didn't seem to indicate anything had gone drastically wrong in town. "Afternoon, everyone. Please take your seats. And thank you all so much for coming on such short notice."

The businessman paused for a moment while a few stragglers hurried to claim seats. "Now, I know you're all wondering what the emergency is. But I'm sure you've also noticed the increased traffic to town this last week." He picked up a small remote and clicked. The screen behind him came to life, showing a chart. "This is, of course, good news. As you can see from the chart here, every hotel and B&B in a ten-mile radius is reporting a significant increase in bookings compared to the last three Septembers. Restaurants and shops are also reporting a corresponding increase in foot traffic and sales. When I noticed the influx of visitors, I went around town, asking as many of them as I could what might account for their presence."

He turned from the chart to face the audience, his grin flashing again. "Nearly all of them reported scheduling a stop on a drive through the area to see the location of *Blackberry Secrets*. Some even came here for the weekend for that explicit purpose, creating a trip around it. And the hotel managers I've talked to said that their reservations for the next several months are increasing as well. Many of those guests mentioned that the book is what spurred their interest."

A buzz of conversation filled the room, though the only individual reaction Hannah could pick out was from Alice, three rows ahead of them. "You mean to tell me that many people are coming here because of a *novel*?"

At the front of the room, Wyatt paused for the commotion to calm down, the overhead light glinting on his gray hair and turning it silver. "I know, I know," he said when he could be heard again. "Hard to believe one work of fiction could really increase the traffic in town by thirty percent. But we've always said that there was more potential for tourism in Blackberry Valley than was realized, if we could lure folks in off the interstate. I think this proves it. Now we have to make sure we handle it well and keep it coming, if we can. Tracy has some ideas."

Tracy Galloway ran an events firm, and her organizational skills and connections had been put to use on the Blackberry Valley town council since well before Hannah moved away. She remembered Tracy from her childhood as a veritable force of nature, and the intervening twenty years hadn't slowed her down at all. If anything, they had just given her more connections.

Tracy flashed a smile at the crowd and scanned a sea of faces that would be entirely familiar to her, even though there were many Hannah didn't recognize. "Y'all know I have been *waiting* for the greater world to discover the hidden gem that is our little town. And now that we have their interest, let's do what we can to keep it. I have here a list of locations specifically mentioned in the novel, which my lovely little helpers are going to pass out to y'all."

Tracy's grandkids, Sage and Taggert, who were somewhere in the eight-to-ten range, began moving down the center aisle with stacks of papers in their arms. They counted out enough for each row, and gave them to whoever sat in the end seat before moving on. Uncle Gordon passed the sheets to Dad.

Hannah set her gaze on the list even as she held out the rest of the sheets to Liam. It was organized into two columns, the first with the historical name of a location, the second with the current name. Places such as *The Reynolds House* in the left column, with *McAfferty Dental and Jackson Chiropractic* in the right.

It was a great list. Living here, she'd been able to piece together a lot of the changes—houses that had been turned into businesses or sold to other families—but even she hadn't been aware of some.

The name *Hanes* jumped out at her from the right-hand column, and she glanced up to scan the room, spotting Claire and her husband not far from where Dad and Uncle Gordon had been sitting originally. Apparently they lived in one of the primary locations in the book, the house from which the buried treasure had been stolen, which had prompted the fictional murder.

Tracy cleared her throat to regain everyone's attention. "As you can see, tourists wouldn't originally be able to tell where each location from the book is. So many have changed hands or been renovated. In some cases, street names have even changed. Unless we want to continue to have people stopping dead in the street from confusion, and causing the traffic jams we've had this week, it would be worthwhile for us to make it easy for them." She waved her copy of the list. "Let's tell them exactly where everything is. I suggest even putting markers at the most important locations. Nothing expensive, just little yard signs like we see for elections that can be pulled up, if and when interest wanes. Or hung, if you don't have soil in front of your location."

"Where are people going to get the list?" someone called.

"We'll have them at a few convenient spots, including the library, Legend & Key, the tourist bureau, and any other business that wants some."

Dad leaned toward Hannah. "You could offer them at the restaurant."

"I definitely could." As a place of business, she certainly didn't mind tourists coming through. But she had to wonder how the private homeowners would feel about it.

Liam must have been wondering the same thing. "Are we really going to direct people to private residences?" His voice projected easily through the auditorium, heads craning around to note who'd asked the very reasonable question.

"As you can see on the list," Tracy said into the mic, "all private residences are marked with an asterisk, and there's a note asking people to please remain outside of fences and to not approach the homes. Nearly all houses mentioned in the book still serving as private residences are notated, so keeping them off the list wouldn't prevent people from seeking them out. But, as long as they're just walking by on the sidewalk, it shouldn't be too invasive. If, however, there are any reports that this behavior *is* invasive, we will of course modify the list to exclude residences. It will be helpful if our homeowners keep us apprised of whether visitors are being respectful."

Hannah glanced at Claire Hanes, whose head was bent toward her husband. She wondered what their opinion was, being the owners of the old Buchanan place, but neither spoke up.

"For those of you who are business owners," Tracy went on, "we invite you to embrace the exposure that *Blackberry Secrets* is giving us in whatever way you can. Restaurants could consider renaming dishes after characters, places, or events in the book. Shops could feature items that have even vague tie-ins. If you're comfortable with the idea, and it wouldn't interfere with your business, those of you in historic locations that were key places in the book could offer tours for a few dollars a head and bring in some extra revenue."

Ideas buzzed through Hannah's mind. The only restaurant mentioned in the book had been a small-town diner that was no longer in operation, but the Hot Spot had some dishes on the menu already that were similar to ones Max had enjoyed. They could absolutely capitalize on that, especially since some of the recipes for those comfort foods had been handed down in Jacob's family.

A grin curved her lips. And she could absolutely feature Hannah Jane Prentiss's cookie jar, with the number of cookies within updated on a mini chalkboard beside it. She bet she could easily find some cookie recipes that had come from her great-grandmother.

"So what you're telling me," a man said from the front of the room, "is that the businesses get to make some extra dough from all this, but those of us who've managed to keep our family homes for the last century have to deal with the hassle of Peeping Toms and curious onlookers clogging our driveways?"

Tracy looked to Wyatt, who returned to the podium. "The tourists are here, Roger," Wyatt said, addressing the man with his easy smile. "We can't change that. What we *can* do is figure out how to manage them and bring some benefit to the whole town."

"I say what we should do is put up No Trespassing signs," Roger groused.

"All around town?" someone else asked. "Way to be as welcoming as your curmudgeon of a grandfather. Stand out there shouting at them to get off your lawn. That way you can make them think you're playing his part."

"At least my grandmother wasn't the town gossip, Jess *Murphy*."

Hannah didn't know exactly how it happened, but that comment seemed to unleash something. Jess Murphy pushed to his feet, clearly ready to defend his family name. Someone else shouted about how Old Murph wasn't nearly as bad as some *other* people named in the book, and from there, it was chaos. Neighbors shouting over one another, accusations and defenses clashing.

Tracy tried to regain everyone's attention—and completely failed. Wyatt took over, shouting, "Calm down!" to little avail.

Dad chuckled and leaned over to say something to his brother.

Hannah exchanged a glance—part amusement, part horror—with Liam. "This thing really has some people hot under the collar, huh?"

Liam smiled. "Veritable fire hazard, from the looks of it."

"Easy for you to say," someone bellowed, the words making it to Hannah from the general din because the woman had turned around to face them. Or rather, to face Alice Tyler. "The Tylers came off smelling of roses! You're probably the one who fed all those lies to the author to begin with."

Hannah had no idea what Alice had said originally to earn that response, but now the elderly woman pushed to her feet. "Ha! I know more secrets about the people in this town than this B.B. Smith character shared, you can be sure of that. And I've half a mind to tell everyone what they are!" Purse in hand, Alice stormed up the aisle and out the door, her granddaughter hurrying after her.

"Wow," Liam muttered. He'd lowered his voice because the din was dying down. Alice's exit seemed to have taken some of the steam from the room.

Wyatt sighed into the mic. "Listen, everyone. I know that this book has dredged up a lot of memories for some of you—things you'd rather forget, in some cases. But I've read the book, and no one comes off all bad. Just real. Instead of being angry at decades-old laundry being aired, look at the fun side. Embrace the fact that our ancestors have become beloved by people all over the country, and not only by us. They'll be *remembered* now. Isn't that what we all want? And how good a job have *we* done of keeping their memories alive?"

Hannah drew in a long breath. He had a good point. She only had a few stories about her great-grandmother in her memory up until now. If she had kids someday, what would she remember to tell them about Hannah Jane? Next to nothing. She'd tell them about her grandparents and parents and her own childhood, of course, but she had so few firsthand memories of Hannah Jane. She was most likely to talk about the people she'd known well.

That was the way of it, unless someone went to the effort of preserving information about generations past. Even then, they could only preserve what had been put down in some form.

Whoever B.B. Smith was, they'd recorded a snapshot of life in Blackberry Valley in 1936. They'd captured the people who lived there in breathtaking, honest color. They'd done what few others could claim to have accomplished.

Tracy stepped back to the podium. "Wyatt's right. Let's honor the memories of our ancestors through this, and be grateful that someone took the time to portray them so vulnerably. I don't know about the rest of you, but I feel like I've been given a gift with this book. Like I got to know my grandmother as a young woman—something I'd never realized I wanted, but it's made me appreciate the woman I knew so much more."

She paused for some affirmative murmurs to ripple through the crowd. "Okay then. I'm going to go through the rest of my ideas, and then we'll open the floor to other suggestions."

Hannah settled in, ready to put on her thinking cap.

Chapter Six

"You know who might have some interesting information on all this?" Uncle Gordon said as he flipped the hot dogs on the grill. "Maeve."

At the reference to his daughter, who was just a little older than Hannah and had always been a good friend and cousin, Hannah looked up from the old recipe box Dad had unearthed from somewhere. "Maeve? Why would she know anything about our family a hundred years ago?"

"Because she's the one who took all those old boxes of papers and junk from the attic when we sold our parents' house," her uncle said, waving his tongs to illustrate his point. "Which had been Grandma Hannah Jane's house before then."

"Oh, yeah." Dad set out the condiments for their Sunday afternoon impromptu picnic. "I'd forgotten we didn't throw it all out. Did she really *keep* all that stuff?"

"She didn't just keep it," Gordon replied. "She went through all of it. Scanned the documents into her computer and everything. I think she might have even put some of it online or something. She posted something about the project a while back, and I meant to go look at what she wrote, but time got away from me."

Hannah returned a recipe card for buckwheat pancakes to the box and reached for her phone. "How did I not know this?" She pulled up her cousin's number and tapped out a quick message. Hey, your dad says you have some historical stuff from the family house and digitized it. Where can I find it?

She set the phone down on the patio table, not expecting an immediate reply. No doubt Maeve was enjoying her own Sunday afternoon with her husband and kids, not hanging out waiting to answer Hannah's random questions. So she turned her attention back to Uncle Gordon. "Do you know what she ended up with? Journals? Newspaper clippings? Scrapbooks?"

"I don't honestly know. Could have been old bills and receipts, or a treasure map or plans for a spaceship. I didn't really look through it. There was so much to sort through."

Hannah chuckled at his list of possibilities. "I'm so sure Maeve scanned in old receipts and put them online."

"Could have," Dad said, easing into a seat with a grin. "Clearly people who write historical novels would lap up that kind of detailed information."

"Good point." She'd wondered how B.B. Smith had found all those small details—or if he or she had made them up and done it so convincingly that Hannah had simply assumed they were accurate facts and not literary license. Or, maybe the author had boxes of family documents too. Surely the old Prentiss house wasn't the only one that would have kept stored records. "But why would Maeve put it online?"

Uncle Gordon shrugged. "You know Maeve. She's always been into anything historical and eager to interest the rest of us in it. And I think she was hoping that if she did a good job on the website she made, it would be a sort of résumé when she put in a bid with the county historical society to redesign their site."

"It must have worked."

Hannah's cousin had been working on that redesign for a couple of months. The last time they'd gotten together, Maeve had been full of stories about how involved the job was and how much she was learning about the area's history as she digitized old documents, records, and other treasures from the archives. She was expanding the website from what had basically been a placeholder with phone numbers to something truly useful to anyone interested in the region's history.

Hannah's phone buzzed, a return text from Maeve popping up. THERE WAS SO MUCH COOL FAMILY STUFF! PHOTOS, OLD REPORT CARDS, JOURNALS, BIRTHDAY CARDS, LETTERS FROM ALL SORTS OF PEOPLE. I SCANNED IT ALL IN AND PUT IT ON A WEBSITE. I'LL EMAIL YOU THE LINK. I'M STILL WORKING SOME BUGS OUT OF THE MOBILE VERSION OF THE SITE, SO I RECOMMEND VIEWING IT ON A COMPUTER. BESIDES, I KNOW YOU'RE HAVING LUNCH WITH DAD AND UNCLE GABE, AND I'M NOT ABOUT TO DISTRACT YOU WITH FASCINATING FAMILY RESEARCH.

Hannah smiled and typed a quick reply. PERFECT. THANKS!

She told her dad and uncle what Maeve said while she went back to the recipe box, the smell of hot dogs making her stomach rumble. She pulled out a recipe for Hannah Jane's Apple Cider Snickerdoodles and beamed. "Score! Not only one of Grandma Hannah Jane's recipes, but it's got apple in it. Spot-on for our seasonal menu at the restaurant." She skimmed the ingredients.

"Doesn't take much to make your day." Dad took the lid off a tub of deli potato salad, sending her a smile and a wink.

"Dogs are done if you want to grab the beans, Gabe," Uncle Gordon announced, deftly scooping picture-perfect hot dogs off the grill.

Dad stood up and moved toward the kitchen door. Hannah took her cue to remove the recipes from the table, securing the ones she intended to copy under the box.

They said grace and dug in, Dad and Uncle Gordon filling her in on news from Maeve's brother, Ryder, and the latest exploits of all the grandkids in the family. Hannah had just seen her brother, Andrew, and his family on Labor Day, but now that all three kids were in school, there was a never-ending supply of new stories—especially since Drew and Allison's youngest, Axel, was proving to be the sort of mischievous kiddo who kept his kindergarten teacher on her toes. Hannah laughed her way through her hot dog, baked beans, and potato salad, sidestepped Dad's question over dessert about whether she intended to spend time with Liam other than sitting together at town meetings, then helped them clean up.

After everything was tidy once more, she stifled a yawn.

Dad sent her a look. "You're going to sleep in tomorrow, right? Catch up on your rest?"

Hannah sighed. "I promised Lacy I'd go out and help with morning chores tomorrow."

"She'll still be doing them whenever you get there, and you and I both know it. Shut off your alarm and sleep in for once. Monday is supposed to be your day to unwind."

"Have you and Lacy been exchanging notes or something?" She bumped his shoulder with hers. "I promise I'll get enough sleep tonight, okay? And Lacy has made me promise that we'll do something fun together soon."

"Glad to hear it. That'll be good for you." He reached for the recipe box and the cards she'd stashed underneath. "Take this home with you and copy whichever ones you want, sweetie. Or keep the whole thing, frankly. It's not like I've been using it. I've tried a few of your mom's recipes from the folder she kept, but I doubt I'll even open this thing again."

She accepted the precious wooden box. "Are you sure?"

"Positive. Take it, use it, enjoy it."

"Thanks, Dad."

"You're very welcome. Now get out of here and go get some rest." He made a shooing motion, and Zeus, who had been snoozing under the table, gave a bark as if in agreement.

Hannah laughed at the dog, leaned down to give him a farewell scratch behind the ears, and exchanged hugs with Dad and Uncle Gordon. "I'll talk to you soon. Thanks for the tip about Maeve having all that stuff from the old house."

By the time she'd driven home, climbed the stairs to her apartment, and deposited the recipe box on the table, she had caught a second wind. Hannah moved to her computer, settling into her chair with a glass of water. Browsing family history totally counted as rest. In her mind, anyway.

Her email held a few messages from Wyatt and Tracy too, no doubt with updates on the tourist-trap planning, but she would ignore those until tomorrow. She opened the message from Maeve and followed the link. She didn't know what she expected, exactly—in her head, scans of family documents would be at home on one of those old-school sites straight from the 1990s—but the beautiful website that greeted her made her jaw drop.

Her cousin hadn't just "scanned junk" and uploaded it somewhere. She'd created a whole experience. There were photos of

Blackberry Valley with captions and dates, pages for journal entries, pages for all those snapshots of daily life that Maeve mentioned—all of it well-organized and showcased in a vintage design that was attractive and easy to use.

She clicked into the *Journals* tab and read the intro Maeve had written.

> *Several partial family journals were stored in my grandparents' old house from various people. There is a childhood diary from my great-aunt in the 1940s, a neglected journal of her mother's, and an incomplete booklet that must have been from someone much further back, presumably preserved as much as it was because it details the family's arrival in the region.*

Hannah's eyes went wide. Her great-aunt's mother must be Hannah Jane Prentiss. "Seriously?" she murmured. They had some of her actual words? Eager to see which years this "neglected" journal covered, she clicked into that one.

And gaped yet again. Not only had Maeve scanned in the pages, which Hannah could download as a PDF, she'd also transcribed them for easier reading. Hannah scrolled through, soon figuring out why her cousin had characterized this journal as she had. There were a few scattered entries for the year 1933, two for 1934, only one from 1935. From what she could see, there was no rhyme or reason for when Hannah Jane decided to pick up her pen again.

Hannah scrolled through the document to 1936, reserving hope that there would be anything from the year during which *Blackberry*

Secrets was set. If the previous trend continued, her great-grandmother would have skipped that range entirely.

But wait. There was an entry from April of 1936. Hannah leaned in to read, her breath catching when the word *cookies* jumped out at her.

> Well, I've gone and done it again. Said something I shouldn't have. And, again, to Annie, who seems to bring out the worst in me, though I don't know why. She was here cleaning today and did a fine job, as she always does. But there's always something a little distant in her eyes, and her parents—well, she's always been a little odd, but it's no wonder, given her family. Still, Bess Adams insists she's the best help to be found, and heaven knows she needs the money. We have a little to spare, so I know it's good to keep her on. I certainly don't mind having less cleaning to do.
>
> But gracious. Something about seeing her stand there, looking so hungry. It gets to me every time, and I snap at her instead of asking her how she's doing. I think Mark's right when he jokes that I'm soft as a porcupine. I prick instead of embracing when things feel vulnerable. Today, I actually told her that I counted the cookies in the jar and would know if she took one. What came over me? Yes, I count the cookies, but not because Annie has ever been anything but honest. More like my own little rascal has figured out how to climb up and snitch them, and then lie through her teeth about it.
>
> Maybe I just wanted to see her reaction. Maybe I was so tired and anxious over this birthday party. I know very well Mark's mother will judge my preparations and find them

lacking, as always. She never says anything, so Mark doesn't believe me, but I know it's happening. Or maybe I just wanted to feel like I was the one in charge in one area of my life. Though if I had to belittle someone in the process, one could argue that I'm far from in control. And one wouldn't be wrong.

I will be better. I still don't know how to respond to my mother-in-law, but maybe I can make strides with Annie, at least. Though I don't understand her, she's surely a respectable young woman, or Bess would never permit her to be Samantha's friend. I should look for the good in her. Be more amiable. Ask if there's anything she needs. Instead of being the snob who looks down her nose at her for her upbringing, I should be the one reminding her that God loves her.

I'll do better. But I'm going to need God to give me the wisdom and help me to be kind when I'm feeling frazzled and unsure of myself.

Hannah leaned back in her chair, staring at the screen. This was the same story as the one in the book, only from Hannah's point of view instead of Max's—or in this case, Annie's.

How was the same story here, and in the novel?

She slapped her hand to her forehead. This was *online*. On a website that used the words *Blackberry Valley* dozens of times, which meant that anyone looking up the town—and probably especially if they used a search term like "1930s"—would likely find this.

B.B. Smith must have stumbled across her cousin's site, read this very journal entry, and changed the facts to fit the story, changing details so that her great-grandmother had interacted with Max, instead of the real-life Annie.

This made sense. Maeve had uploaded all the documents a while ago. Probably while the author was writing the book.

Did that mean that the other stories in the book were also discoverable online? If so, then it meant the author *didn't* have to be local. Anyone, anywhere, could have learned about the cookie story online. Which meant they could possibly learn about others.

She hadn't taken notes specifically about the stories verified by her neighbors, but the book was still fresh enough that, by glancing down her list of families and how they were portrayed, she remembered the particular stories that brought them to life. She'd just enter some of the key search terms with *Blackberry Valley* and maybe *1936* and see if she got any hits.

Twenty minutes later, Hannah was beginning to doubt her own ability to do an internet search. An hour later, she had new respect for any author who put in the time to research things this much. Two hours later, she had a crick in her neck and had found exactly one other story shared in an online source. On one hand, this was frustrating, but on the other, it was fascinating. The story had also mentioned someone by the name of Annie. A young Jeremiah Miller had dropped a full can of milk when he spotted his older sister kissing Freddie Sanderson, though she was engaged to Freddie's brother. Annie had helped him clean up the mess.

Leaning back in her chair, Hannah rolled her head to try to loosen her neck. She didn't know what the common character signified, though it surely meant something. And the discouraging thing was that finding only one documented story didn't prove the others weren't out there somewhere too. All it proved was that she hadn't yet landed on the right search terms to find other anecdotes, or put in the hours.

And she wouldn't be able to. She wasn't a writer. She was a restaurateur who had to focus on her actual job, and a friend who'd promised to take a break tomorrow and go out to Lacy's farm. She would have to accept that this particular idea had yielded about as much as it was likely to.

But she had learned something. Her great-grandmother really had counted the cookies in the jar, and it was someone named Annie, not Max Stuart, to whom she'd said such a thing. Hannah assumed it was the same Annie who had helped Jeremiah Miller clean up his spilled milk. She didn't know how this information would lead her to B.B. Smith, but it still felt significant.

Pushing away from her computer, she decided to set the mystery aside for now. She would get a good night's sleep, go play with some goats in the morning, visit with Lacy, and see what other ideas came to her. Perhaps the break would give her brain time to come up with fresh ideas.

And yet she tossed and turned in bed for a while before finally drifting into an uneasy sleep.

Chapter Seven

Blackberry Valley
April 10, 1936

If one focused on architecture and furniture, then the Buchanan house was, without question, Annabeth's favorite house in all of Blackberry Valley.

It wasn't the largest—that prestige went to the Adamses' place, which was an actual mansion. But the Buchanans' Queen Anne-style home had such *character*. Gingerbread swirls on the exterior trim, charming gables and garrets, pretty wrought iron flourishes on the peaks of the roof, and even a turret. A *turret!* What could be more perfect?

And the inside was every bit as appealing. All the rooms featured gorgeous plasterwork, and some even had murals on the ceiling. The floors were patterned wood that was so lovely she actually enjoyed polishing it every week. In this house, Annabeth could pretend she was a heroine of ages gone by—though, given the way Mrs. Buchanan always snapped at her, the most fitting story was *Cinderella*.

But never mind that. She hummed as she made another pass over the parquet, ignoring the protestation of her knees. They'd feel better after she stood, stretched, and walked to the next job—the *last* job of the week, and one that made her grin. Not that the job itself made her grin, but the Adamses did.

She'd get to see Sammy, which was always the highlight of any day it happened. And Sammy's younger siblings would clamber over her, making her laugh. Mrs. Adams would tut that she was too thin and insist she stay for dinner. And even though she was there to clean, the work was always light, because the Adamses were the only family in town that employed a full-time housekeeper. Sue Ellen did most of the cleaning throughout the week, and Annabeth dropped by to help with the bigger tasks. Even though Sue Ellen didn't ever really *need* her assistance unless it was to help prepare for some big event.

It was a pity job. Annabeth knew it, but she couldn't afford to turn it down. And she didn't want to. Sue Ellen always greeted her with genuine gladness, saying how happy she was to have the help for an afternoon. The family all treated her like an actual person instead of someone to be ignored when she wasn't being commanded. Even Mr. Adams's dog greeted her with a wagging tail.

How was it that the richest family in town was also the nicest? From the books she'd read, that wasn't the typical way.

"Are you about done in here, Annie? Mr. Buchanan will be home soon for lunch."

She looked up to see Mrs. Buchanan in the doorway of her husband's study—the floor of which was Annabeth's current work. "Very nearly, ma'am." She gave the woman a smile, trying to ignore her irritation at being called *Annie*.

They all called her that, all the women who employed her. Despite the fact that when she'd knocked on their doors and offered her services, showing them Mrs. Adams's recommendation, she'd introduced herself as *Annabeth*.

She knew why they all did it—because that was what Mrs. Adams called her. But, coming from her best friend's mother, it was an endearing nickname carried over from childhood, one she scarcely noticed. Coming from everyone else, it felt like a deliberate attempt to belittle her.

No doubt she was reading too much into it, and it was her own insecurities gnawing at her. Which was why she'd never corrected any of them. And so, she had no one but herself to blame, not really.

Mrs. Buchanan nodded. "See that you're out of here before his arrival. You can always finish up afterward."

"This is my last task, ma'am, and I should be done in five minutes."

The lady sighed and checked her watch. "That will be cutting it close, but I suppose there's no help for it. Finish up as quickly as you can. I'll leave your pay on the kitchen table."

"Thank you, ma'am." She went back to work while the lady was still standing there watching, making a show of quickening her speed. A pace she kept up because, honestly, she didn't fancy being caught in the office by the man of the house either. Not that Mr. Buchanan had ever been anything but coolly polite when their paths had crossed, but still. They weren't all as bighearted as Daddy had been, nor as kind as Mr. Adams.

But it was better to think about the house than the man who owned it anyway. She was still sorting out the motives for murder in her story, but whatever they were, this house ought to feature in at least one of them. Maybe her schoolmarm could be staying here. The house couldn't belong to her, as a newcomer from Nashville, but the schoolmarm might be boarding with the family. That would work. They could have school-age children.

The Buchanans had two adult children, both older than Annabeth. The daughter was married and lived in Louisville, and the son worked with his father. The family had moved to town eight years before, which meant that Annabeth had never interacted with either of those grown children in the town's little one-room schoolhouse—assuming they'd even have sent their children there. The Adamses hired a tutor for Sammy and her siblings, and it seemed probable to Annabeth that the Buchanans would have done something similar for status. But her story version of the family could have fictionally aged versions of Cora and Edwin, who attended the town school. Then it would be reasonable that the schoolmarm would reside with them.

She finished the final corner, dropped her rag into the bucket, and stood just as heavy footsteps sounded in the hallway, approaching the door. She spun to face the entrance as the two Misters Buchanan both entered, their conversation pausing as the elder caught sight of her.

Embarrassed heat crept up her neck, even though she had no reason to be ashamed at being caught cleaning the study. She was doing her job, and it wasn't as though she'd been slow about it. But her flushes always seemed to defy logical explanation. The familiar warmth would climb from her neck to her cheeks and ears, leaving splotchy redness in its wake whenever it felt like it.

The elder Mr. Buchanan cleared his throat. "Good day, Miss Billings."

"Good day, sir." She directed the greeting to the father, nodding at the son as well. "I was just finishing up in here." With this, she edged a bit closer to the door, hopefully making it clear that they were blocking her escape.

Mr. Buchanan strode to his desk and set his briefcase on top, not so much as glancing at her again. "Very good. Have a pleasant afternoon." He was already flipping open the latches on his case.

"You too, sir." She took another step toward the door then halted with a frown.

Edwin Buchanan hadn't budged from his place, which meant he was still blocking her way. And looking at her. With a hand held inexplicably out. "Let me help you with that bucket, Miss Billings. It must weigh about half as much as you do."

For a moment, she could only gape. No one—*no one*—offered to help her with her scrub bucket. Why would they? She had clearly been hefting it around all morning, up and down the stairs, as he must know. He was, after all, in business with his father, and their mill and woodworking enterprises had been so successful in Louisville that they'd come here to open a second branch and bought this house.

But still he stood there in her way, hand out expectantly.

Annabeth gripped the bucket more firmly. "Thank you, Mr. Buchanan, but that's not necessary. I'm quite capable."

When he smiled, a dimple made its appearance in each of his cheeks and light sparkled in his blue eyes. "I don't doubt your ability. But my mama raised me to be a gentleman and help a lady with her burdens." He took a step closer, reaching for the bucket.

No one in Blackberry Valley had ever called her a *lady*. And Mrs. Buchanan might have raised him to be a gentleman, but Annabeth had a feeling the lady of the house had never intended for her son to offer assistance to the hired help. But he was now close enough that Annabeth could smell the spice of his cologne as his fingers curled around the bucket's handle.

She glanced at his father, quite certain he'd have a scowl on his face and would be ready to tell his son to leave her to her scrub bucket. But Mr. Buchanan was ignoring them altogether. He'd apparently taken a few stacks of cash from his briefcase and stood now at the massive safe in the corner of the room, spinning its dials to open it.

The bucket's weight lifted, and she let go rather than wrestle with him over it. Her gaze snapped to the young man, who was still smiling at her as if—well, as if she were Samantha Adams or Prudence Tyler instead of Annabeth Billings.

Victorious, he took a step back toward the office door. "Where were you headed with it?"

"The kitchen." Not knowing what to do with her hands now, she wiped them on her apron. She followed Edwin as he left the office and made his way to the kitchen.

"Have you always lived in Blackberry Valley?" he asked as they walked, his tone friendly and warm.

Proving he *hadn't* always lived here. No one other than Sammy's family and Pru—who had only become her friend because Sammy had introduced them as children, though by now they were a close-knit trio—ever talked to her like this. "All my life, yes."

"Do you have any siblings? Are your parents still with us? I can't recall meeting any other Billingses in town."

Her throat went tight. "Mother passed away five years ago, Daddy just a few months back. No siblings."

He paused in the kitchen doorway and cast her an apologetic look. "I'm so sorry. You must miss them terribly."

She nodded, blinking back tears.

His dark brows drew together. "I can't recall ever meeting your parents."

Because they hadn't been able to afford any of the fine wooden toys or furniture or even raw lumber that the Buchanans produced. "Mother never came to town. She was deaf and had a difficult time communicating with people. And Daddy..."

His brows rose. He still stood in the doorway to the kitchen, the bucket in his hand, looking at her as if she were any other girl.

It was best to go ahead and tell him why he shouldn't. Her chin edged up. "He had a port-wine stain birthmark that covered half his face."

To her surprise, his features softened. "I know people often judge things that make them uncomfortable. I imagine he had a resilient spirit as a result."

It was a good thing she wasn't carrying the bucket because she might have dropped it in shock. When she recovered her powers of speech, she said, "He did. He had to."

There had been some who had not approved when Mother and Daddy married, insisting that two people with issues like they had shouldn't be allowed to have children. Those people seemed to think that physical deformities meant there was something wrong with Daddy on the inside too, and they were the ones who'd long ostracized him because he didn't look right.

Edwin's face and voice remained kind and gentle, but not pitying. "That some people judge others based on appearances never ceases to make me sad." He finally turned back toward the kitchen. "The sink?"

Annabeth had to swallow a smile at the mental image of his mother's face if she dumped dirty scrub water down the pristine sink. "No, I dump it outside." She decided not to dwell too much on his fair-minded words. Plenty of people held such opinions in theory. But somehow, it had been different when they were actually looking at her father. Then their theories rarely manifested as practice. "And really, sir, you don't need to do that for me—"

"It's no great task. I've been sitting at a desk all morning, so moving around feels good." He flashed her another smile and pushed through the screen door onto the porch. A moment later, the sound of water sloshing onto the bushes filled the air. When he reentered the kitchen without so much as a splash mark on his fancy suit, he added, "And you don't need to call me 'sir.' I'm only a few years older than you, by my estimation."

It wasn't age that made her offer the respectful address. It was status. And the fact that if his mother caught her calling him anything *but* "sir" or "Mr. Buchanan," she'd have something to say about it.

As if summoned by the very thought, Mrs. Buchanan strode into the kitchen and immediately frowned. "What's the meaning of this? Edwin, what are you doing with Annie's scrub bucket?"

Edwin set it down, all innocence. "Just helping her empty it. It looked heavy, and she looked tired."

Thunderheads gathered in the woman's eyes. "She looks the way she always looks—perfectly capable. I do not hire help so that you can help *them*. Now go wash up. Lunch will be served in a few minutes."

Rather than appearing chided, Edwin said, "If she always looks so tired, then perhaps more people should offer to help."

Annabeth barely kept her mouth from falling open.

He turned to her, head inclined. "I hope you have a good afternoon, Miss Billings."

"*Annie*," his mother hissed, the correction obviously meant to remind him that the *help* didn't warrant respectful address.

Annabeth couldn't have said what came over her, but she knew Edwin Buchanan was somehow to blame for the way her spine straightened. "Actually, I prefer my full name, which is Annabeth."

Edwin's lips twitched into a smile. "Noted. Good day, Annabeth."

That wasn't what she'd meant—an invitation for him to call her by her first name. That felt strange and too friendly.

His mother clearly agreed, given the scowl she turned on her. "I believe you're finished here for the day, aren't you, *Annie*?"

Annabeth reached for the money on the table, quite certain this would be the last time she would have the chance to earn any in the Buchanan house. "Yes, ma'am." She paused, waiting for the dismissal. The order not to come back.

Instead, Mrs. Buchanan said, "Come earlier next week, so you're finished before the men return for lunch."

Her shoulders wanted to sag in relief, but she kept any reaction from showing. "Yes, ma'am." She made her escape, dashing out into the spring sunshine.

It had to be Mrs. Adams's doing. That was all she could think as she hurried toward the mansion on the hill. She must have somehow made it clear to the women in town who all looked up to her that they weren't to dismiss Annabeth. Several of them sure seemed to want to, but they didn't.

How had Sammy's mother done it? Annabeth knew she should be grateful, but it made her feel like more of a charity case than ever.

Chapter Eight

Blackberry Valley
April 10, 1936

As Annabeth neared the Adams estate, she spotted Pru Tyler bicycling in her direction, clearly coming from the house. Pru stopped beside her with a smile. "Hey, Annabeth."

"Hey, Pru." She nodded toward the mansion. "Giving the twins their piano lessons?"

"Yep. Say, I had an idea I wanted to run by you. Sammy's birthday's coming up, and you know how she complains about the stuffy, formal parties her mother always plans, especially since it's so close to their annual dinner dance. What do you say we come up with something more fun for her instead? A picnic or something?"

Annabeth's brows hiked up. "Instead? You know her mother's not going to give up her party. We could probably do it in addition to the party, but—"

"But you know Sammy said the only gift she wants is to get out of that party." Pru grinned and batted her lashes. "And while *I* don't dare suggest such a thing to her mother, *you* certainly could."

Annabeth laughed. "Right. As if she'd listen to me."

"She adores you!"

Mrs. Adams did have a soft spot for her. Annabeth couldn't deny that, despite the fact she couldn't explain it. But even so... "I doubt her affection for me outweighs her love of throwing a party. But I'll see what I can do."

"That's all I ask." Pru repositioned her handlebars. "I have to get to my next lesson. See you Sunday?"

"Absolutely. Have a great day, Pru." Annabeth waved her friend on and continued up to the house, entering through the kitchen door where Sue Ellen was bustling about the stove, no doubt getting the Adamses' lunch ready for the table. "Hi, Sue Ellen."

The housekeeper tossed a smile her way, perspiration gleaming on her forehead. "Hi, honey. I made you a sandwich."

Another reason why she loved her days helping here. She'd long ago given up arguing when Sue Ellen foisted food on her. "Thanks." She ate quickly while Sue Ellen got the meal set in the dining room and the family's footsteps thumped down the stairs. Part of her wanted to slip out and eat with Sammy, but she resisted. It wasn't as if Mrs. Adams would object, but

Annabeth knew if she did that, she'd end up lingering and talking instead of actually helping with the chores.

Annabeth was keenly aware of all she owed this family and was eager to do *something* to pay them back. So she'd help with the housework *first* then go and find her best friend.

Sue Ellen made it easy to forget she was working, though. She saved the two-person tasks, like moving the rugs outside for beating and folding the large sheets and blankets, for days when Annabeth was there to help her, and they went about the tasks with laughter and stories.

Before she knew it, the last of the chores were done and Sue Ellen was shooing her out and toward the stairs. "Get on up there and have your girl gossip. I know you've been itching to see Sammy since you got here."

Annabeth found her best friend at the sewing machine in her room, cheerfully hemming a skirt that Annabeth knew would be donated to the church's perpetual clothing drive. Most people gave their cast-offs or hand-me-downs, but not Samantha Adams. She spent her time making pretty new garments and then slipped them into the donation bin anonymously.

Annabeth flopped down on Sammy's bed with a happy sigh at the softness of the mattress. "You know," she said over the hum of the machine, "if you let Reverend Cassidy actually *see* you donating so much to the various funds and drives, I bet he wouldn't keep having Sunday dinner with the Jeffersons."

Sammy sent her a playful glare. But she was fighting a dreamy smile, as she always did at the mention of the handsome young minister who had come to Blackberry Valley two years ago. Every young woman in town had set her sights on him, it seemed, but no one else was quite as subtle about it as Sammy. "I am not doing this to get his attention."

"Obviously not, since you've been doing it since you learned to sew." Annabeth rolled onto her side to better view her friend. "But you're not doing *anything* to get his attention, despite wanting it so badly."

And her friend wanted that attention for good reason. Reverend Cassidy was a fine man. Annabeth might have been tempted to have a few dreams about him herself, if Sammy hadn't so quickly developed a crush on him. And if she weren't keenly aware that she'd merely bring down the reputation of a man like him, which wouldn't serve him well.

Sammy stuck her nose in the air. "I refuse to flaunt myself about like Victoria or Rose or Emily."

They'd had this conversation a dozen times, if not more. "I'm not saying to flaunt yourself. I'm just saying that you're a bit intimidating, and he might need some assurance that you're interested before *he* shows any interest."

Sammy finished her hem and rolled her eyes. "I am *not* intimidating."

Annabeth snorted. Not only was Sammy from the wealthiest family in the area, but she was also beautiful and held herself with the sort of confident grace that she must have been born with.

Sammy shook out the skirt and stood, holding it up to herself. "What do you think?"

Annabeth nodded her approval. "Beautiful, but practical too." Unlike most of Sammy's dresses, which were solely beautiful. Practicality was seldom required for an Adams.

Sammy folded the garment in half and draped it over the ironing board she kept ready beside her sewing machine. Rather than iron it now, though, she moved over to sit beside Annabeth on her bed. "How was work this morning at the Buchanans'?"

"Oh my goodness. You'll never guess what happened!" Annabeth filled in her friend on the events of the morning, including Edwin helping with the scrub bucket as well as his mother's reaction.

Though it was hardly a thrilling escapade, Sammy's eyes went obligingly wide. "Edwin Buchanan defied his mother for you?" She pressed a hand to her heart, trapping a stray golden curl beneath her palm. "Oh, how romantic! He's nearly as handsome as Reverend Cassidy."

And a far better match for Sammy. Annabeth hadn't missed the many attempts Mr. and Mrs. Adams had made to throw their eldest daughter into the company of the Buchanan heir, but Sammy neatly sidestepped nearly all of them. Because, as she'd told Annabeth years ago, "He doesn't inspire any dreams in my heart." It seemed only humble ministers with hearts of gold could do that.

At her friend's comment now, Annabeth shook her head. "There was nothing romantic about it. It was strange. That's all."

Giving her a look that said she was being a dunce, Sammy smacked her arm with a small pillow. "There is nothing strange about a young man helping a pretty girl."

Annabeth squirmed at the easy compliment but knew better than to argue with it. "I don't know. He must have had some kind of ulterior motive. I bet his mother has been badgering him about settling down, and it was his way of pushing back. Or he was trying to distract me while his father put all that money in the safe."

Now Sammy's expression called her silly and cynical. "Sometimes people are just nice, you know. It's called doing the right thing."

Not many. Not to her. Not often. Annabeth shrugged. "People like your Reverend Cassidy, sure. People like the Buchanans?" She shook her head. She'd love to make generalizations about how people with money didn't need to be nice, but here she was in the biggest house in town, beside her richer-than-anyone best friend, who utterly disproved the point. So she kept her mouth shut.

Sammy beamed at her. "I think he's taken with you. He's probably been watching you for months, straining for a glimpse of you, trying to figure out what to say, when finally there you were in his father's home office."

It was Annabeth's turn to smack Sammy with the pillow. "Ridiculous. And kinda creepy. He's been *watching* me?" She made a menacing face like a villain from one of the movies they'd seen together.

Sammy laughed. "Not like *that*. You're far too eager to cast everyone as the villain in your murder mystery. Speaking of which." She leaned closer, eyes gleaming. "When are you going to let me read what you're writing?"

"When it's worth reading."

"Annabeth," Sammy protested.

"Not yet, okay? It's still too rough." And still bore the names of all their neighbors. Amusing as that was for Annabeth, it would lead to endless lectures from Sammy. "But I *will* let you read it at some point. When I'm finished."

Sammy hugged the pillow. "Fine. You can make it up to me by spending the night and helping me watch the twins. Mama and Daddy are attending a dinner in Cave City tonight and won't be home until tomorrow."

"I'll stay until you get them put to bed," Annabeth countered, "but then I'd better go home so I can close up the chicken pen for the night."

The evening passed in the usual fun that came from spending time with Sammy and her nine-year-old siblings, Cordelia and Cornelius. The twins ate dinner and played games until their favorite radio show came on, took their baths, and then snuggled in around Sammy for another chapter of the book she was currently reading to them.

When the twins were younger, Annabeth actually felt helpful when she stayed like this—wrangling the two of them at age six had been quite an ordeal. But these days, they were calmer and only half as mischievous, and it was more a delight than any kind of work. They settled into their beds with only a few protestations, and Annabeth made her way to the back door with a sigh at the thought of the long walk home.

"Are you sure you don't want to stay?" Sammy asked, peering out into the darkness. "I don't like the idea of you walking home alone at night, and I know Mama wouldn't either."

"I'm out at night all the time. I'll be fine." Annabeth gave Sammy a hug. "I'll see you Sunday." She didn't linger long enough for her friend to launch another argument for why staying was wiser than going. It was too tempting, and she really should shut up her chickens for the night. She'd only had them a few months, and they'd just started laying. It would be a shame to lose them to a fox or a raccoon.

The night air was cool, her thin cardigan doing little to protect her from it, but Annabeth made up for it with a quick pace that would warm her in no time. A brisk walk often helped her put story pieces together, and she'd been eager to let her mind wander back to her book all evening. She liked the idea of using the Buchanan house as a setting, but now she would have to decide how much the Buchanan-equivalent characters were involved in the nefarious doings. As the schoolmarm's hosts, they were too obvious to be the actual villains, but suspicion should still start there. Max was too logical to ignore it, though too clever to be blinded by the obvious.

She glanced toward the house in question as she passed it on her way out of town, to cement in her mind the image of it on a lovely moonlit night. That turret silhouetted against the sky, the wind whistling through the gingerbread trim. All the lights were out already, though it was only half past nine, making her wonder if the Buchanans had gone to Cave City tonight for that dinner too. Surely they weren't all in bed already.

Then the town was behind her, and the country road stretched out ahead, promising that she'd be home in one more mile.

A minute later, a strange sound cut through the night, one that made her slow her pace reflexively. It almost sounded like a shovel. Cutting into the earth, scooping the soil, then the thud of that earth being dumped elsewhere.

But who in the world would be shoveling at night? Out here, away from town?

Cold dread slithered through her. Maybe Sammy accused her of searching for exciting stories in the mundane, but even she would have admitted that this was bizarre. And here was Annabeth, standing on the road, illuminated by the moonlight, there to be seen by whoever was out here doing heaven knew what.

She scurried to the side of the road, into the protective cover of the trees. Her action served the dual purpose of hiding her and putting her closer to the sound. Wisdom ordered her to slink away in the shadows and hurry home, staying unseen by whoever else was out there, lest it *was* someone going about something nefarious.

But curiosity had always been one of her biggest faults. She followed the sound instead, though she was careful to stick to the shadows of the trees lining the road. She crept through them until she could see the field on the other side—and the figure laboring away at the earth, digging a hole at the base of a thick old oak.

His white shirt all but glowed in the moonbeams, and even from where she stood, she could tell it was a young man by the way he moved. His hair appeared dark, and when he straightened, she saw he was tall and thin. As she watched, he lifted a wrist to wipe at his brow then tossed the shovel aside and reached for something on the ground. It looked like a box, and it must have been metal, given the squeak and clang, like a handle rattling against the top.

He—whoever it was—was burying it—whatever it was. Which was curious at best and alarming at worst. Why would someone be out in the darkness, burying a box? Unless it was something stolen. Or illegal. Or something even worse, somehow.

She didn't mean to ease back a step, didn't realize she had until a twig snapped under her foot, as loud as a gunshot in the stillness of night.

The man snapped upright, and she saw the moment he picked her out of the shadows. Recognition lit his features just as sure it did her own mind.

With a gasp, Annabeth flew out of the trees and sprinted full speed back the way she'd come. She didn't dare head toward home and lead him straight to her little cabin. She would be all alone, and there'd be no protection there. No, she made a beeline for the Adams house, ignoring the hissed, "Miss Billings! Annabeth!" that came to her ears along with the thundering footsteps that told her he'd given chase.

But Annabeth had always been a good runner, and her daily labor kept her fit and strong. Whether it was because of that, because an office job had left him out of shape, or because he'd realized he couldn't chase her into town without raising suspicion, the footsteps behind her soon faded to nothing.

She didn't once look over her shoulder. No, she'd watched enough movies and read enough books to know that it was when someone fell prey to that temptation that they stumbled and fell into the clutches of a madman. She'd keep her focus straight ahead and pour all her energy into speed.

Her caution paid off. He didn't pursue her through the quiet streets of town and certainly not through the gates of the Adamses' property. She told herself that was because he'd given up, rather than that he had decided to bide his time and catch her later.

She paused at the back door, chest heaving. She would have to catch her breath before she roused Sammy to let her in. She wasn't about to tell her best friend what she'd just seen, and if she came in flushed and panting, Sammy would definitely ask questions. She wasn't ready for that. Not yet.

Because if Edwin Buchanan was up to no good, then who knew what he'd do to protect whatever secret he'd been burying? Annabeth wasn't about to drag her best friend into a real-life crime in progress.

Chapter Nine

Hannah stepped out into the warm September morning and took a moment to breathe in the fresh air before moving to her car. She'd gotten a good night's sleep, as she'd promised her dad she would, even if she *had* ended up with a few unsettling dreams in which a faceless woman named Annie constantly hovered out of view. Hannah had known she was there, but could never manage to catch more than a glimpse of a faded vintage dress, no matter how quickly she spun.

Her phone chimed with an incoming text, and she paused to check it, finding a new message from Lacy.

I will love you forever if you stop at Jump Start and get me one of the autumn spice lattes Zane just added to the menu.

Hannah grinned. How long will you love me if I add an apple fritter?

Three forevers! And would you have time to swing by the bookstore? Neil accidentally grabbed one of my seed order forms with his stuff and I need it. The sale ends today.

I thought you ordered everything online.

Yeah but I like to look through the physical catalog, so I list out what I want on the form then go online to order it.

I SEE. DO I GET FOUR FOREVERS FOR THAT?

FIVE, ACTUALLY. I AM VERY GENEROUS WITH MY FOREVERS.

Laughing, Hannah promised to pick up coffee, pastries, and order forms and be at the farm as soon as she could. A few minutes later she pushed open the door to the café, savoring the aromas of coffee and sugar that greeted her as she entered.

She smiled when she saw Claire Hanes at the counter, a to-go cup in hand. "Oh, hey, Claire. It's like we both love this place or something."

The woman smiled and lifted her cup in salute. "So much better than what I can make at home. Grabbing a cup a few times a week is one of my indulgences."

"I try to limit myself, but I'm here on a mission of mercy today. I'm going out to my friend Lacy's farm, and my mother raised me never to show up empty-handed."

Claire chuckled. "A true friend."

"I try. Hey, I saw you and your husband at the meeting on Saturday. I didn't realize you live in the Buchanan house. You haven't been mobbed by tourists or anything, have you?" She'd hoped to check in with them on Saturday, but once the meeting finally dismissed, it had been too chaotic. And of course, Alice and Jules had already stormed out, so Hannah hadn't gotten a chance to question them either.

Claire shrugged. "We've noticed some people walking by we didn't recognize and some slow-moving vehicles on the street. It would be alarming if we didn't realize what was going on. Fortunately, no one's actually come onto our property or anything. Although…"

At her hesitation, Hannah lifted her brows. "Although?"

Claire sent her gaze out the window, crossing her arms over her chest. "I'm not sure I like this new map idea. It's one thing to say on a list that the house is a private residence, but it's quite another to show people exactly where it is."

"Map?" Hannah hadn't heard anything about a map, though she'd checked her email that morning.

"Yeah, Wyatt called us last night to say he'd just had the idea and wanted to run it by us—since our house is of more interest than the other private residences. It's basically what it sounds like. A map of the town that highlights the locations in the book."

"Huh." Hannah shifted out of the way of another customer headed for the door. "I mean, that's cool on the one hand, but I absolutely understand your concern. I hope you told him your thoughts."

Claire rolled her eyes, a bit of a smile on her face. "I didn't have the chance. My husband, Josh, seems to think this is the most fun ever and told Wyatt to go ahead. He loves all this. Of course, he's more of a people person than I am. He spent half the weekend hailing every tourist who came by and talking with them about the book. I had to put my foot down when he said we should offer tours."

Hannah laughed. "I would have too. I mean, I don't mind extra attention for the restaurant, but I'd feel differently about my home. My apartment is upstairs from the restaurant, of course, but that feels different somehow."

"Josh keeps insisting that I'll get it when I finish the book, but I still have about a third to get through. I'm beginning to feel very behind the times, but whenever I sit down to read, my boss texts or one of the kids needs something or I'm falling asleep." She took a sip of her coffee.

"I finally finished it over the weekend. Great book, I have to say. I thought the treatment of all the real families was really well done," Hannah said. "No one is perfect, but that's true to life, isn't it?"

Claire smiled then reached into her pocket when her phone buzzed. "There's my boss, right on cue. I'd better get home so I can get back to work. Good seeing you again, Hannah."

"You too. Have a great day." Hannah proceeded to the counter and placed her order, exchanging hellos with a few other locals. While she waited, she noticed a couple studying the menu long and hard. They must be visitors. Minutes later, Hannah was out again with Lacy's order in hand, along with a coffee for herself.

She hurried to the bookstore and went inside, coming to a halt a few steps from the counter when she saw Wyatt Granger there with Neil. A map of Blackberry Valley was spread on the counter between them.

Neil greeted her with a smile. "Hey, Hannah. Lacy said you'd be stopping by. Let me go grab her stuff."

"Thanks." As he turned to the back room, Hannah nodded to Wyatt. "Morning, Wyatt. I just ran into Claire Hanes. Is this the map she mentioned?"

He tapped his finger on it. "Yep. Neil's offered to help me with it, since he's our resident expert on such things. We've decided to use a vintage style like this one, but he's going to add little drawings of the buildings for places of interest. What do you think?"

"Sounds fun." She moved closer to the counter so she could see the map. Neil had also sketched what he must have envisioned for those buildings on a separate sheet of paper. "I'll be happy to keep some of these with the lists in the restaurant, of course."

"Oh good. I wasn't honestly sure what your stance was on the book, what with your great-grandmother being mentioned. I thought she came off very realistically and positively by the end, but I've been pretty surprised by some of the reactions around town."

"Me too, honestly." She leaned against the counter. "I actually felt like I got to know her better through the book. I loved the experience."

Wyatt nodded. "That was how I felt too. I couldn't believe the hullabaloo at the meeting. I thought people would be excited. I mean, who'd have thought that we'd actually see such an uptick in tourism so quickly?"

"It's something we should count as a blessing. Though I understand why the affected homeowners might be more hesitant."

His gaze became thoughtful. "Fair point. But I'm hoping if we make it clear that they're welcome to drive or walk by and instruct them to respect the privacy of the residents, they'll behave themselves."

Though she hoped so too, Hannah couldn't resist a grin. "I don't know. The descriptions of the Buchanan house certainly made *me* want to see the inside of it."

Wyatt chuckled. "From the sound of it, Josh Hanes wouldn't object. Poor Claire might though. I think he's trying to talk her into hosting an open house for us locals."

Claire hadn't mentioned *that*. Hannah shook her head. "I mean, I'd love that, but it sure would be a lot for Claire to manage."

"I know. And if he does, I bet folks will start wondering if he's the author."

Hannah concurred. People would probably wonder, but she couldn't be certain. Claire wasn't acting as though she had any inside knowledge about the book, and surely if her husband had written it, she'd have read it already.

Neil reemerged from the back, waving the order form his wife had requested. "Here it is. Thanks for ferrying it to Lacy."

"No problem at all." She took the form from his hands and lifted a hand in farewell. "Have fun with your map, gentlemen. I'd better get Lacy's latte to her while it's still hot."

She started toward the door, pausing for a second when one of the patrons browsing the bookshelves caught her eye. The woman seemed familiar—platinum-blond bob, sharp cheekbones, stylish shirt and capris, probably in her mid-thirties—but Hannah couldn't think of a name. Had she visited the restaurant? It was possible, but that backdrop didn't seem to go with her face.

Hard to say. Probably just someone she'd seen around town, and since the woman was studying the books before her and not looking up to exchange pleasantries or even vague smiles, Hannah shook it off and continued out of the shop.

The drive to Bluegrass Hollow Farm passed quickly, and soon Hannah parked and scooped up the things she'd brought for Lacy, wondering where her friend was at the moment.

She didn't have to wonder long. Lacy strode out of the barn with a wave, her auburn hair glinting in the sun. "Perfect timing. I just finished up and was heading into the house for a break. Let's have coffee, and then you can visit the animals."

"I was supposed to help you with chores." She handed over Lacy's latte and order form, carrying her own cup and the bag of treats.

"You did. You ran errands so I didn't have to. And while we enjoy our coffee, you can tell me all about this meeting I missed on

Saturday and how your hunt for B.B. Smith is going." Lacy waggled her brows. "Have you uncovered her secret identity yet?"

"Her?"

Lacy shrugged. "The writing felt more emotionally driven than I expect from male writers."

There had been a few times Hannah had thought the same—and then other times, she'd been sure B.B. must be a man. "I don't know. I could lean either way on that one. And no, I haven't made any progress on the author's identity. Although you'll never guess what I found last night in some old documents my cousin uploaded." She explained everything as they settled at the kitchen table and pulled out the apple fritters, including how she'd gone searching for other stories from the book and only found one—but that it had also featured a character named Annie.

Lacy's eyes went wide. "That's something, right? Some clue?"

"Maybe? I'm not sure what it's a clue to, exactly. But it certainly seems too interesting to be coincidence. I just don't know how the same woman being present at two different events in the 1930s helps me figure out who wrote this book today."

Lacy silently chewed the last bite of her fritter then licked the sugary glaze from her fingers, her expression contemplative. "Maybe this Annie person wrote it all down too and left her own journal. Someone from her family could have been the one to write the novel."

Hannah gaped at her. "That's actually a brilliant thought."

Lacy gave an exaggerated bat of her lashes. "Why, thank you." Then she narrowed her eyes playfully. "Though you don't need to sound so surprised."

"Not how I meant that 'actually.'" Hannah swirled her coffee and took another sip. "Though if that's true, we're back to the writer being a local. Or at least someone whose family is from here. I guess that doesn't mean *they* still live here. Plenty of locals move away."

"True. But I don't know how we'd prove this theory, even if I'm right. I mean, it's a sound idea, but pure conjecture."

Hannah tapped her finger on the table as she let the idea simmer. "I think the first step would be trying to figure out who this 'Annie' person even was. If we can find a record of her from the time in question, then maybe we can figure out who her descendants are. It would be a starting place."

"Maybe try those census records you said you were already looking at."

"Seems like a good place to start." And there were other clues about Annie in Hannah's journal entry too. The reference to being "allowed" to be friends with Bess Adams's daughter indicated that the daughter—and therefore probably Annie—were young enough to still be living at home. And of course she knew that this Annie was hired to do housework. If she worked for multiple families, including the one from the other story Hannah had found online, that could account for how she had learned details about them and their homes.

Did that mean that Annie would know whether one of those families had had money go missing? Could she even know where it was buried? If such a thing were true, though, why wouldn't she just have dug it up herself and returned it to the rightful owner?

"I've lost you," Lacy observed with a grin. "What's swirling around in that head of yours?"

Hannah blinked, refocused on her friend, and shared her musings.

Lacy considered it all. "From everything I've read, privileged people were rather famous for being so good at ignoring the hired help that they let a lot of secrets slip in front of them. That could be at work here." She grinned. "As for the buried treasure, there's only one way to tell. We need to go find that oak tree and start digging."

Hannah laughed. "An oak tree outside of town, right off the road. That ought to be easy to find. We'll have Neil and Wyatt put it on their map."

"What map?"

Neil must not have had a chance to tell her yet. Wyatt probably hadn't run it by him beforehand, just stopped in this morning to talk about it in person. "Wyatt's planning a map of all the book locations for tourists."

"So he went to Neil. Oh, he'll have a blast with that." Lacy drained the last of her coffee. "We could go treasure hunting for our girls' night out. Bring a metal detector and a picnic. Spend an evening scanning every oak tree along the road."

"And hope the big old one from a hundred years ago is still standing? Sounds like a blast." Hannah finished off her coffee too and stood to throw away the cup. "A saying about needles and haystacks springs to mind."

"Or, I saw a post on social media about a concert in Cave City on Saturday. That's an option."

Hannah grinned. "Not sure how that's going to help us find the alleged buried fortune."

Lacy chuckled and tossed her own trash. "Girls' night, silly. Keep up."

"A concert could be fun. That goes on the short list. Or we could go see that new rom-com that opens on Friday."

"Things to consider." Lacy moved to the sink to wash her hands. "Ready to visit the goats?"

Hannah clapped her hands together. "More than." When she got home, she'd go back to census records and buried treasure. For now, she had some cute little animals to play with.

Chapter Ten

Hannah dashed into the bank on Wednesday morning, the Hot Spot's deposit bag tucked under one arm, her attention on a text message from the restaurant supply company. Her recent order of straws was on back order, and it would be another week before they shipped. She was trying to remember how low they were and to decide if she needed to make a trip to a store to tide them over, when she plowed into something.

Or rather, someone. "Whoa there," Liam said, his strong hands catching her elbows to steady her.

Heat stung her cheeks. "Oh, I'm so sorry! I know better than to walk and use my phone at the same time."

He was grinning, clearly not injured by her recklessness. "Putting out fires?"

She smiled back. "I'll leave that to you. I'm chasing down drinking straws."

"Are they running away?"

"Out of stock temporarily, with my supplier." She held up her phone as evidence then slipped it into her pocket. "Was that a new recruit I saw sitting with you guys last night?"

Liam and a few other firefighters had come into the Hot Spot the previous night, but she hadn't had a chance to say hello before they'd gone. It had been another busy shift, full of inquisitive visitors who had been grateful for the book location lists she offered. In fact, she'd had to bring out more halfway through the evening.

But she'd been curious when she saw a young woman sitting beside Liam at the table of firefighters. She hadn't seen a female firefighter before but loved the thought of one joining the ranks.

"What?" Clearly *not* a new recruit, given the confusion on his face. Though it cleared in the next moment. "Ah. No, that was Bryn. She likes to wear the department T-shirts to support her boyfriend." One corner of his mouth quirked up.

To her surprise, Hannah's stomach twisted. So what if Liam had a girlfriend? It wasn't as if Hannah had any claim on him. She didn't have time for a relationship, as she repeatedly told those who kept trying to set her up with eligible bachelors. If Liam was happy with someone, then, as his friend, Hannah was happy for him.

Or, so she told herself.

"I think it's sweet that she's there for you in that way," she told Liam, hoping her smile wasn't as strained as it felt.

Liam's confusion returned. "For me?"

"I mean, I'm sure she supports the other guys too, but of course she'd be there mostly for you, right?"

"Why, because I'm the chief?" Liam asked. "I guess I could see that if she weren't dating Archer, but he's definitely her favorite."

Hannah's mind cleared. Archer Lestrade was Liam's best friend and fellow firefighter. Now that she thought about it, he had been sitting on Bryn's other side.

"That would explain how comfortable she looked beside him." She decided to gloss over the miscommunication before either of them read too much into it. "I saw the post online yesterday saying you're going to conduct a controlled burn of that old barn on the Riggleman farm as a training exercise, so I thought maybe you had new people to train."

"There'll be some trainees from the volunteer fire department in Park City. 'Controlled burns' always come with a bit of risk, and I'm really hoping we have it all wrapped up by midafternoon on Saturday. So say a prayer that all goes well, if you think about it."

"Of course I will. What's with the deadline? Big plans Saturday night?" Hannah could have kicked herself. It sounded like she was fishing for information on his personal life—perhaps even his *dating* life—which she certainly wasn't.

Or didn't mean to be.

If it bothered him, he didn't let on. Just flashed that handsome smile of his. "Hopefully. I told Gramps I'd take him to the Apple Festival on Saturday night."

"Apple Festival? Here?" How had she not heard of this?

"Well, not in town. It's at the county fairgrounds, though tons of people from Blackberry Valley go. It's all weekend. They have food vendors, crafts, live music, games—all apple-themed, of course."

She lifted her brows and grinned. "Even the music?"

His laugh rang out. "Okay, *most* things are apple-themed. If you've never been, you should make time to go. You're welcome to come with me and Gramps if you want."

Was he asking her out? Obviously not. No guy asked a woman on a date with his grandfather, though Hannah had met Patrick and enjoyed his company. He was inviting her to see a regional event as a friend. So he wouldn't mind if she deflected. "Actually, Lacy and I have been searching for something to do this weekend for a girls' night. That could be perfect. Is it still happening on Sunday?"

"They close at six on Sunday. That's our backup plan if things don't go well at the burn. And the closing concert is usually amazing, so it's a great time to go." Still smiling, he shifted toward the door. "Maybe we'll see you there."

"I hope not." Hearing how that sounded, she widened her eyes and hurried to add, "I mean, for your sake! I hope the controlled burn doesn't go badly enough to make you resort to your backup plan. Obviously, I wouldn't mind seeing you there. And you know I love your grandfather."

Liam laughed as he pushed open the door. "I'm going to tell him you said you hoped not to see him. See ya."

"Bye." She waited until he'd exited then pressed a cool hand to her warm cheek. What was wrong with her?

Glad the bank lobby was empty of other customers who might have overheard their embarrassing conversation, she shook her head and strode to the teller's counter. It only took a few minutes to make her deposit and exit again, slip in hand. Once settled back in her car, she paused to send a text to Lacy. WHAT ABOUT THE APPLE FESTIVAL AT THE FAIRGROUNDS FOR GIRLS' NIGHT? OR GIRLS' DAY?

THAT'S THIS WEEKEND? HOORAY!

SO SAYS LIAM. I TAKE IT YOU ENJOY THIS FESTIVAL?

IT'S AWESOME! WE SHOULD ABSOLUTELY GO ON SUNDAY. YOU'LL LOVE IT. AND LIAM SAYS, HUH?

Hannah rolled her eyes. DON'T READ INTO IT. I RAN INTO HIM AT THE BANK. LITERALLY. She'd save the story of her faux pas for an actual conversation rather than a text. No doubt Lacy would roll with laughter over that one.

WHATEVER YOU SAY. WE SHOULD GO AFTER CHURCH, EAT LUNCH THERE, AND WANDER UNTIL IT CLOSES AT 6. AS LONG AS I BRING NEIL AN APPLE DUMPLING, HE WON'T MIND IF I ABANDON HIM ALL AFTERNOON.

SOUNDS LIKE A PLAN. CAN'T WAIT.

She couldn't remember the last time she'd wandered around a festival for hours on end. There'd been a few vendor events in California, but that had been more work than fun, as had the Blackberry Festival in town the previous month. Maybe a state or county fair when she was a kid? The Apple Festival certainly hadn't been going on then, or Mom would have insisted they attend.

She and Lacy would have so much fun. And getting it settled and on the schedule relaxed something in Hannah as she returned to the Hot Spot. Once there, she double-checked their straw supply and decided they could wait the extra week for the shipment—though they'd be cutting it close. She replied to the message from her vendor. A few other bookkeeping tasks claimed her attention, but she cleared them all out in less time than she'd anticipated and found herself with a handful of minutes and nothing work-related demanding her attention.

Might as well get back to the census records. She'd spent some time with them the day before while she had her breakfast before diving into work for the day. She'd hit a roadblock almost immediately. With no surname to help her out and far too many names that "Annie" could be a nickname for, she had too many possibilities.

Hannah had started making a list of every female in the county with a name beginning or ending with Ann. Little did she know how common a name it was. And without a birth or death year to narrow the search, how would she ever find the mysterious Annie?

Many of the names didn't make it onto her list when the data provided immediately ruled them out—either their age or circumstances. The census data told her not only the names of each person, but whether they owned a home, the value of the house, who their parents were, etc.

The Annie she was looking for surely hadn't come from a wealthy family, if she was being paid to help clean houses and if Hannah Jane had described her as having a "hungry" look. That pointed to someone from more modest means, and if she and Lacy were right that Annie was a younger woman, that ruled out many more of the listings.

But there was so much Hannah didn't know. Was Annie married? Had she been living with her parents? Was she in Blackberry Valley proper at the time, or from somewhere outside of town?

Jacob popped his head into the office. "Hey, boss. The cookies are ready, if you want to load the new jar."

Pushing thoughts of Annie aside, Hannah stood with a smile. "I do indeed."

In the kitchen, Jacob had a variety of individually wrapped cookies on a tray, their new, giant cookie jar waiting beside it. Hannah washed her hands and began layering the oversized treats into the wide-mouthed jar. Of course, she counted them as she put them in.

Once finished, she carried the jar out into the dining area and positioned it beside the chalkboard that stood ready and waiting. Raquel, who had the best handwriting among them, had already written *Hannah Jane Prentiss's Cookie Jar* in pretty script on the board and was now adding a list of the flavors Jacob had baked. The server looked to Hannah with lifted brows. "What's our count?"

"Thirty-two."

Raquel wrote the number in the big circle she'd already made on the board.

Hannah clapped her hands together. "I love this."

Leaving Raquel to finish up, Hannah turned her attention to other tasks that needed doing. As always, the minutes flew by, and four o'clock was soon upon them.

She loved seeing customers already lined up outside—though, much like the last two days, she didn't recognize any of the eager faces. As she switched on the Open sign and unlocked the door, a welcoming smile settled on her lips. She pulled it open and said, "Hey, there. Welcome to the Hot Spot. Hope you're hungry."

"Famished," the woman at the front of the line said as she and her companion moved inside. "We've been walking around your pretty downtown all afternoon, pretending we're characters in *Blackberry Secrets*."

The man beside her shook his head, amusement in his eyes. "*You* were pretending. I was making sure you didn't walk into traffic when you spotted a familiar shop name across the street."

Hannah laughed and ushered them to Elaine at the hostess stand. "Well, I'm glad you worked up an appetite—and that no one walked into traffic."

The woman was already squealing, a hand to her chest. "Oh my goodness! Hannah Jane Prentiss's cookie jar! Honey, we have to get some cookies."

Elaine pulled out two menus and nodded to Hannah. "Our lovely owner here is none other than Hannah Prentiss—great-granddaughter of the Hannah Jane you know and love."

The woman spun to face her, eyes wide. "No way!"

"Way. And we used Hannah Jane's cookie recipes too." Jacob had made a few tweaks—he couldn't resist, and Hannah couldn't argue with the results—but they were close enough to still feel like Hannah Jane's cookies. An extra dash of cinnamon or using real butter instead of "oleo" didn't change that. She'd had to laugh when Dylan had asked what on earth oleo was and what it was doing in cookies, then at his headshake when Jacob had explained that it was an old-fashioned term for margarine.

Although, according to Jacob, that last question was valid even when one did know what it was.

"I want one of each flavor," the woman declared as she turned to follow Elaine.

"And she'll probably eat them as an appetizer, so go ahead and bring them over," her husband added.

"Your server, Raquel, will bring them," Elaine assured the couple.

The early success of the cookie jar buoyed Hannah through the next hour. When she spotted Wyatt stepping inside with a stack of papers in hand, she detoured to intercept him. "Did you see Hannah Jane Prentiss's cookie jar?"

He beamed at the sight of it. "Brilliant. Are you counting the cookies that go in and out?"

She motioned toward the chalkboard, which currently read twenty-eight. They'd already topped it off once, as room was made for what hadn't originally fit.

Wyatt laughed. "I love it. And here are the maps."

"Already?" She reached for the glossy prints he held out to her. "That was fast. And they're beautiful." Rather than cheap black-and-white versions, they were in full color and had a watercolor style, each starred location depicted by one of Neil's full-of-character drawings.

"Jim Comstock and Neil worked together and got the files to me this morning. Turned out great, didn't they?"

"Fabulous." Her eyes went on a quick visual tour of the illustrated town. "These are going to go like hotcakes. I hope they weren't too expensive."

"The print shop gave us a good deal on them, given the circumstances. We started with a thousand. If we run out, then we know something about the number of people coming through." Wyatt angled back toward the door. "I've got more to deliver. If and when you run out, let me know and I'll drop off more."

"Will do. Thanks." She continued to marvel over the maps as she set the stack of them beside the location lists they'd already been handing out. She couldn't believe how quickly they'd produced such fine work. But Wyatt had clearly known exactly whom to go to. No one in town knew maps like Neil, and of course the bookshop owner would be eager to promote this book-related tourism. He had a huge display of *Blackberry Secrets* in the shop.

In fact, of the places in town that stood to benefit financially from an influx of tourists, Neil was in a sweet spot. He had a direct connection to the book as a bookseller, the display of which was sure to invite in anyone who came to town for that purpose, at which point he could recommend similar titles or local-interest books. She wouldn't be at all surprised if he was selling maps like these, only on heavier paper ready to be framed and mounted. He was probably on cloud nine over there.

Then she went still. Hadn't Lacy mentioned a while back that Neil was writing something in his spare time? It made all the sense in the world, given his profession. The man loved books as much as he loved maps. He knew what went into making a good one and probably had connections in the book world from the shows and conventions he went to. He had a whole section in the shop on local history, to say nothing of his many perfect maps of Blackberry Valley.

Her phone was in her hand before she'd thought the notion through, her finger swiping out a hurried message to Lacy. HEY, DIDN'T YOU SAY A WHILE BACK THAT NEIL WAS WRITING SOMETHING?

The dots bounced. Stopped. Bounced again.

Which was when Hannah realized how that question would sound to Lacy. How her thoughts, while logical in one respect, were utterly wrong in another.

A point which Lacy clearly didn't miss.

SERIOUSLY? YOU CAN'T ACTUALLY BE SUGGESTING WHAT I THINK YOU ARE. YES, HANNAH. HE'S BEEN WRITING A FANTASY NOVEL. DO YOU HONESTLY THINK WE'D LIE TO YOU? IF AND WHEN NEIL GETS PUBLISHED, HE'LL BE CROWING AT THE TOP OF HIS LUNGS, NOT WRITING UNDER SOME PEN NAME AND KEEPING IT A SECRET. AND THAT WOULD BE BECAUSE HE WOULDN'T BE AFRAID FOR HIS LIFELONG FRIENDS AND NEIGHBORS TO KNOW HE'D WRITTEN SOMETHING, BECAUSE IT WOULDN'T AIR THEIR FAMILIES' DIRTY LAUNDRY FOR THE WHOLE WORLD. I CAN'T BELIEVE YOU WOULD THINK THAT

OF HIM. OR OF ME, THAT I'D MARRY SOMEONE WHO'D DO THAT. THANKS, HANNAH.

Hannah's eyes slid shut, her breath gusting out. What had she been thinking? She ducked into her office and called her best friend. She had to make this right.

At first, she was afraid Lacy wouldn't answer. Finally, an icy, "Yes?" came down the line.

"You're right, Lacy. I'm so sorry. I didn't think it through that far. I just knew he loved books and must be a talented writer. I didn't consider the content of *Blackberry Secrets* with Neil's character at all. Can you forgive me?"

There was a long sigh. "Yes. That's what best friends do. And it was my idea for you to dig into this whole mess in the first place. Plus, I don't think I ever mentioned to you what kind of book Neil is writing. Your question just surprised me, that's all."

"I completely understand. It won't happen again," Hannah assured her.

When they hung up a few moments later, Hannah was at peace once more. But she also felt a new resolve to be more careful. After all, the whole reason she felt the need to investigate this was to make right the harm being done to innocent people's reputations by some of the cruel behavior of characters in the book—even if most of them turned out to not be all good or all bad. It made her no better than the author if she did the same thing by pointing fingers at whoever happened to pop into her mind.

Chapter Eleven

Hannah dropped the cookbook into the library's return bin on Saturday morning, but her attention wasn't on the library as much as a plume of black smoke billowing up in the east. Even though she knew exactly what it was—the controlled burn of an old barn on the Riggleman farm several miles outside of town—it still made her pulse ratchet up a bit.

She knew the firefighters were out there with their hoses and equipment, and she could still hear Liam's words in her head. Controlled burns came with risks. Old boards could fall in unexpected ways. Trainees might make mistakes—as might veterans whose attention strayed for a moment. They could do everything right, and yet the fire had potential to take on a life of its own.

A good reminder to do as Liam had requested and say a prayer for the safety of him and his team, as well as the volunteers from Park City.

After her silent amen, she turned back toward the parking lot and saw that someone was sitting on one of the benches outside the library. Claire had a copy of *Blackberry Secrets* beside her, but the book was closed, and the woman was staring off into the distance.

Hannah took a few steps closer, her brows knitting at the expression on Claire's face. She couldn't quite read it. Wistful? Thoughtful? Sad? Upset? Whatever the right choice of description, she couldn't simply walk by. Perhaps they were acquaintances rather than real friends, but she'd always believed God put people in one another's paths for a reason. Maybe she'd felt the urge to return that cookbook today so that she'd see someone who needed her. "Claire? You okay?"

Claire started, blinked, and focused her gaze on Hannah. But the smile she offered still held that same combination of expressions. "Hi. Of course."

"You sure?" Hannah perched on the end of the bench. "You don't seem okay. Is it the tourists?"

"No, no one's been any trouble." But Claire sighed and leaned back against the bench. Her gaze dropped to the novel at her side. "It's the book."

"Oh?" Was Claire maybe the type of person who felt things very deeply when she read a story?

Rather than answer right away, Claire seemed to be gathering her thoughts. She moistened her lips then finally met Hannah's gaze. "The part in here about the Ratchfords—that's my family."

"The Ratchfords." Hannah mentally went over the list she'd made of all the characters, but she came up blank. "I'm sorry, but I don't remember where they were in the story."

"Just a few passing mentions, really. The big one was about how Gracie was sent to the sanitorium."

"Right! And we'd seen Gracie a few times beforehand. Max had noticed her chapped hands and how she was constantly picking at her scalp, as if she was nervous. He'd wondered if she felt guilty. One of the red herrings."

Claire nodded, staring off again. "I've seen pictures of Gracie. I resemble her, so I asked who she was. And my grandfather got super quiet and said they didn't talk about his aunt much. That she had tuberculosis and was sent to a special hospital but never got better." She looked at Hannah again. "B.B. Smith tells a different story, doesn't he? She wasn't sent away because she had tuberculosis. She was sent away because she had a mental illness. He makes that very clear and calls the Ratchfords out for lying about it."

Hannah frowned. "Chapped hands and an itchy scalp don't mean—"

"Not itchy—just picking. And chapped from over-washing." She lifted her own hands, which were red and chapped. Hannah had never noticed that before. "I think she must have had obsessive compulsive disorder, given the things Max observed and described." She gave a laugh that sounded a bit too shrill to be believable. "He could have been describing *me*, Hannah. And my daughter, Callie, who's in the library right now." She bit her a lip for a moment, as if to stop it from trembling. "She's been picking at her scalp lately. I changed her shampoo, thinking, like you said, it was itchy, but now I don't think that's it. I think we have this same illness that my grandfather's aunt had. I passed it on to Callie without even knowing, and now I feel so careless."

Hannah prayed for the right words to say to her friend. "Behavioral health and our understanding of it have come such a long way since then, Claire. It's certainly nothing to be ashamed of. There are so many amazing things our brains and bodies do every single day that something is bound to go awry every so often."

Claire blew out a breath. "I know you're right. I'm more amazed that I had never put it together. I never stopped to think that everyone doesn't act the way we act. Not until I read it in this novel and saw myself in her, and had Max say so plainly what my family always denied—that they always *lied* about. And how does that denial help anyone? We could have gotten tools and assistance for this so long ago." She shook her head, lifting a hand to wipe at her eyes. "I'd love to say the author was the one making things up, but how can I, when I can see those same symptoms in us today?"

Hannah had no response to that. She leaned back against the bench and let it sink in. Because she would have been inclined to say the author was taking artistic license for the sake of the story—using a family who had a member shipped off to a hospital and making it more interesting, ascribing motives and even symptoms to them that weren't really there. All to make Gracie, who had been hoping to become the teacher at the schoolhouse, a suspect for a few chapters.

But the fact that Claire and Callie had the same symptoms made Hannah's inclinations moot. Sometimes OCD had the potential to carry a genetic component, didn't it? She had a friend in California who had it, as did her friend's dad and grandmother. Zoe had been diagnosed first, as a teenager. It was only after they'd seen how medication and therapy had changed her life that her other family members realized that they had been self-managing the same symptoms all their lives—and that they could get help too.

Zoe had been very open about it, and about the ADHD that went along with it in her family. It was part of their family psychology, and while some of it needed to be properly managed in order to allow them to truly thrive, other parts were *how* they thrived. Zoe used the hyperfocus that came along with her ADHD to get things done, and the attention to detail from the OCD helped her excel—as long as she could stop when she needed to and turn her projects in. It was merely the explanation behind some of her unique gifts, as well as some of her unique struggles. And when Hannah thought about it, everyone had both gifts and struggles. It reminded Hannah to give grace to those whose explanations she didn't happen to know.

But in the 1930s? The study of mental health had been in its infancy, and some doctors had performed horrible experiments on patients who suffered with things that could now be treated with medication and counseling. Hannah had caught a few documentaries on asylums and had been shocked not just at what they were doing, but how long those practices went on. Some of those places hadn't been shut down until the 1960s or even later.

But she hadn't had a personal connection to any of the patients before. "You really think your great-great-aunt was sent to one of those places?"

Claire lifted her chin. "I do. I'd always wondered about Grandpa's claim about the tuberculosis sanatorium. There was something in his eyes when he said it, you know? Something guilty and full of regret. I thought it was because he knew his grandparents were sorry they hadn't kept her at home, but this makes so much more sense. If she had symptoms visible to someone outside the family, I know she must have had even more that she didn't cover up at home. Things my family must have been alarmed by and ashamed of."

Hannah's chest ached for the whole family. "It carried such a stigma back then."

Claire turned to face her, her expression shifting from vulnerable to determined. "Which then makes me wonder how anyone today could possibly know. How could someone know this about

Gracie, when my family has lied about it for the better part of a century?"

"I have no idea," Hannah admitted. "Maybe someone came across her name in an old record at the place she was sent? But why would someone even be looking?"

"I couldn't begin to imagine." Claire released a breath and shook her head. "I guess it's possible. But it feels more like someone saw her for themselves, you know? Someone saw Gracie's behavior. Someone saw how her family reacted. Someone saw her go away for good and probably heard the stories they told—that she was sick in the body, not in the mind—and they wrote down the truth."

Someone saw. A shiver slid up Hannah's spine. Maybe the same someone who had heard Hannah Jane Prentiss say she counted the cookies in the jar? Maybe the same someone who had helped Jeremiah Miller clean up the milk? "Annie."

"Who?"

"You know the story in the book about my great-grandmother and the cookie jar? My family has an old journal of Hannah Jane's where she tells the same story from her perspective. But it's not Max in her kitchen. It's someone named Annie, hired to clean. And an Annie was mentioned in another story from the book that I found online. I wonder if she kept a journal, wrote all this stuff down, and someone inherited it and turned it into the novel."

"That sounds far more reasonable than someone today unearthing all these old details one by one." Claire's face brightened. "I wonder if Annie wrote anything else about Gracie. I want to know what happened to her. I mean, I'm kind of afraid to find out. I've seen some horrific things about those old mental hospitals. But still. I feel so close to her right now. She's helped me see something in myself, in my daughter. Something we can get help for now that I recognize it. I feel like I owe her. And the author, or this Annie, or whoever."

Just like that, Hannah had a reason to appreciate B.B. Smith, who had offered much-needed, though painful, knowledge that could now be used for good. She reached over and gave Claire's chapped hand a gentle squeeze where it rested on the bench between them. "We'll figure out who the author is and where they got their information."

Claire gave a wry grin. "I don't know. If I were B.B., I'd be pretty eager to keep it a secret after that meeting last week. There are a lot of people who aren't exactly happy with the author."

"Well, maybe we need to encourage whoever it is to come clean. Get people to share their positive reactions more openly, to offset the negative ones." She could certainly share how she felt like she knew her great-grandmother better now. Maybe add to the Hannah Jane Prentiss Cookie Jar display. She could get a framed photo of Hannah Jane as a younger woman, about the age she was in 1936, to put up beside it. And she could write up a short bio about her from her perspective as the great-granddaughter of the character, perhaps even include Hannah Jane's side of the cookie story. She could publicly thank *Blackberry Secrets* and its author for helping her get to know her great-grandmother better.

Claire's next long exhale sounded almost peaceful. "Maybe I should let Josh host this open house he's so gung-ho about. Even if we never know who the author is, it feels like a way to thank them for writing this book. And maybe if we all try to be a little more like Max and notice these things so we can grieve with those who grieve and rejoice with those who rejoice, it could make a difference."

Hannah nodded her agreement. "That's exactly what the author invites the reader to do too. I hadn't put my finger on it."

"But you did it. Here, today." Claire sent her a warm smile. "Thanks for stopping to talk and help me work through my feelings. It was all swirling around in my head, and I was having a hard time with it."

"I'm glad I happened to be walking by. I felt like I was butting in, but I had to make sure you were all right."

"I'm glad you did." Claire peered at her. "And, at the risk of sounding like I'm butting in, you've looked rather tired whenever I've seen you lately. I hope I'm not out of line here, but I hope everything is okay."

Funny how Hannah could dismiss the evidence when Dad pointed it out, but couldn't argue when it came from someone she barely knew. "Yeah, I should probably make more of an effort to prioritize rest. Set aside some time each day when work isn't allowed to steal my thoughts. And I do have a fun day planned with Lacy Minyard on Sunday. We're going to the Apple Festival."

"Oh, our family loves that! We're going tonight."

Claire's statement sent Hannah's gaze back to the sky and the still-rising plume of dark smoke. She said another prayer that all would go well with the fire, and the firefighters would all be safe.

The library door opened, and Claire called, "Hey, sweetie. All done?"

Callie approached their bench—scratching at her head. Hannah wouldn't have thought anything of it, had it not been for the preceding conversation. The girl smiled at her mom and hoisted her tote bag higher on her shoulder. "Yep, all stocked up. And they had the latest book in that series I'm reading."

"Awesome. We better get home so you can get started on it." Claire stood, gathering her book and sending Hannah another smile. "So good to talk to you, Hannah."

"You too. If you do have that open house and need a hand with anything, let me know."

Callie's mouth fell open. "You're seriously thinking about it, Mom? That would be so cool! All my friends at school are *dying* to see our house."

Claire laughed and put a hand on her daughter's shoulder to steer her toward the parking lot. "We'll see, but I'm leaning that way. Bye, Hannah."

"Bye." She kept her seat for a moment while the Haneses walked away, letting the conversation settle. Along with Claire's final concern for *her*. Hannah hadn't thought she was pushing herself too hard, but clearly everyone else could see something she hadn't.

It reminded her of Max, the amateur sleuth who saw his neighbors so clearly. It made her wonder about Annie, and whether the mysterious woman from nearly a century ago could possibly be his real-life counterpart. It made her wonder about B.B. Smith.

Which in turn made her think about Lacy, who was clearly still peeved at her for thinking for even a moment that the author of *Blackberry Secrets* might be Neil. After a day or two of few texts, Hannah had called her friend to reiterate that she'd just let her thoughts carry her away without really pausing to think it through fully, that she *knew* Lacy and Neil wouldn't keep something like that from her. Her friend's words had offered forgiveness, but her tone had said it still irked her. Unfortunately, Hannah couldn't take back the words.

She pulled out her phone and sent her best friend a text. WE'RE STILL ON FOR TOMORROW EVEN THOUGH I'M AN IDIOT, RIGHT? I'M REALLY LOOKING FORWARD TO IT.

It took a minute, but eventually the dancing bubbles indicated that Lacy was replying. Finally, the response popped up on her screen. OF COURSE. YOU KNOW I LOVE YOU FOREVER. EVEN WHEN YOU'RE AN IDIOT.

Hannah smiled in relief then glanced over when the library door opened again. A woman emerged, her hair in a sleek blond bob, stylish sundress matching perfectly with a handbag that was definitely designer. She pulled out a pair of sunglasses and slid them on.

The woman from the bookstore. Not a huge surprise if a booklover went to the library as well, but as Hannah looked at her now, dressed as she was, she could suddenly place where she'd seen her before.

On her television, when she'd tuned into the regional news. The blond woman was one of the anchors on the Louisville station's morning show. What was her name? Hailey? That sounded right. Hannah couldn't remember her last name, but her certainty about the woman's identity grew when she watched her walk into the parking lot and climb into a BMW. There were a couple of those around town, but none so new.

For a long moment, Hannah kept her seat on the bench. What was a news anchor from Louisville doing in Blackberry Valley for days at a time? In the bookstore, in the library, where the historical society kept their records and displays?

The timing couldn't be a coincidence, could it? Hailey had to be here because of the novel. Maybe she was going to do a human-interest story about the book and its real-life setting, covering how the novel's success was impacting the town. Or perhaps she was here as an investigator, trying to find out the same thing so many of them were—who B.B. Smith really was.

Hannah pushed to her feet and started toward the library instead of her car. She might not be a trained investigative journalist, but no out-of-town reporter was going to beat her to the punch.

Chapter Twelve

Blackberry Valley
April 25, 1936

A branch creaked in the gusting wind, and Annabeth jumped, scanning the yard outside Sammy's window for anything moving that shouldn't be. She saw nothing out of the ordinary, but that didn't mean Edwin Buchanan wasn't out there.

He was there far too often, every time she turned around. Five times in the last two weeks, he'd nearly caught up with her. Cornered her. She'd managed to evade him, but in a town the size of Blackberry Valley, it was only a matter of time.

She'd been rather proud of herself for managing it so far without losing the work at his family home. She'd sent a note around saying when she'd show up, but had come at a completely different time. It had frustrated his mother, but it had also meant the house was empty of everyone *but* Mrs. Buchanan, which was all she cared about.

"What is wrong with you?" Only Sammy could ask such a question of her with affection to match the clear accusation. She moved into place beside Annabeth at the window, peering through the glass for herself. "You've been jumping at shadows for weeks. What did you see that night you came back here to stay?"

Annabeth's fingers fell away from the curtain she'd been holding, as if it scalded her. "What do you mean?"

Her friend shot her a look. "Don't play dumb with me, Annabeth Billings. No coyote howling in the woods would scare you like that. You saw something, and you're still spooked about it. I've been waiting for you to come clean on your own, but I'm starting to doubt that you ever will. So stop hiding it from me already."

It was on the tip of her tongue to deny it yet again, but then she made the mistake of looking into Sammy's green eyes. And she saw the hurt there, over Annabeth keeping a frightening secret. She saw the concern. She saw the reminder that Sammy was one of the few people left in the world who truly cared about her, and Annabeth wasn't giving her the chance to be there for her like she wanted to be.

That was the sort of thing that could ruin a friendship—and if this one crumbled, the one with

Pru would probably be close behind, because why would Pru choose Annabeth over Sammy? And without those friendships, what did she have?

Nothing. Nothing but a typewriter that Sammy had given her, empty cupboards, and some cleaning jobs she'd never have gotten without Mrs. Adams's recommendation.

She sighed and sank onto the window seat. "You're right. It wasn't an animal. It was a person."

Sammy grabbed her hand, eyes wide. "Who? Did someone hurt you—or try to?"

"Not at all. I wasn't hurt in any way, I promise." She gave her friend's hand a squeeze. She wanted to assure Sammy that if she'd been injured, she wouldn't have kept it from her. But Annabeth wasn't sure that was true—didn't know how far she'd go to keep Sammy from getting involved in something that could be dangerous. So she stuck to what she knew was true. "I saw something that someone didn't want me to see. When he spotted me, I ran here. He followed for a while but gave up when I reached the edge of town."

Sammy's eyes went wider with each sentence, her grip tighter. "Who? And what did you see?"

Annabeth squeezed her eyes shut for a moment. She knew that Sammy wouldn't believe her. Why would she? Annabeth could scarcely believe it herself. Since the Buchanans had come to Blackberry Valley eight years before, they'd been nothing but upstanding citizens. They'd invested in the town and quickly taken their place at the top of society. The parents were already pillars of the community, and Edwin was a sought-after bachelor all over Kentucky. She'd seen invitations to balls and galas and dinner parties in their house from Louisville, Lexington, Bowling Green, and more.

"Annie, you know you can trust me. Right?"

Annabeth peeled her eyes open. Coming from Sammy, the childhood nickname caressed rather than grated on her. Soothed a few rough edges inside. "Of course I do. It isn't that. It's that if he's involved in something criminal, you could be in danger by knowing."

Sammy clasped Annabeth's fingers so tightly she briefly feared that they might snap. "Okay, now you're scaring me. *Tell* me, Annie!"

Annabeth dragged in a long, shaking breath. "It was Edwin Buchanan. He was in a field outside of town, burying something."

Sammy's eyes bulged. "Like a *body*?"

"What? No way! Where do you come up with such ideas, Sammy?" And that was something, wasn't it? If someone were burying a body, that meant they had likely killed and would kill again. Like the cold-hearted villain in her story. "It was a metal box. I think he must have stolen something." Just because someone was a thief, that didn't mean he was a murderer. It was more probable that he'd try to buy her silence rather than ensure it through violence. Bribery would seem like a safe bet with someone like her, wouldn't it? She was clearly poor. Edwin must believe that the offer of money would be enough to guarantee her cooperation.

But when she refused his hush money, what then? What would that drive him to? That was why she'd been evading him. Things would escalate once they had a confrontation. And escalation meant danger. Anyone who'd ever read a mystery knew that.

Sammy's grip eased. "That doesn't make sense. The Buchanans aren't hurting for cash. They're doing a booming business, and Edwin is the heir to it all. What would he have stolen?"

"Do you think having money insulates people from greed?" Annabeth tugged her fingers free so she could stand to pace the room. "Your family is the exception, Sammy, not the rule. Trust me. In my experience, those who have much always want *more*. And they'll stop at nothing to get it."

"Well, did you go back at any point to see what he'd buried?"

And that was why she loved Sammy—well, one reason. She was so quick to abandon her own objections and just believe Annabeth. "Not yet. Every time I've walked by it, there's been someone out working the fields. I considered coming back after dark one night, but—"

"But that would have been foolish." Sammy leapt up and bounded over to her wardrobe. "We'll go now. The field hands always get Saturday afternoons off, along with Sundays. And if it's on the other side of that copse of trees, we shouldn't have to worry too much about being spotted from the road."

"You can't mean to go with me to search for it." Perhaps they'd galivanted through the countryside as children, hunting for adventure that they'd had to fabricate when they failed to find any in reality, but Sammy was a lady now. From her perfectly curled hair to her pristine heeled pumps. To Annabeth's horror, she kicked off those fine shoes in favor of the old boots she'd unearthed from the bottom of her wardrobe. Annabeth's brows rose. "Those *can't* still fit you."

Sammy grinned and held the boots up. "My feet haven't grown since we were twelve, thankfully. Now to find those old trousers."

Despite the situation, Annabeth laughed. "Your mother will have a fit."

"Oh, nonsense." Sammy set the boots down and went back to digging through the armoire. "She'd have a fit if I ruined one of my dresses. But she won't mind at all if we go for a little hike through the countryside, especially since there's no reason to tell her *why*. It'll be good for my health or something. Aha!" She pulled out a pair of decade-old trousers, grabbed a blouse, and moved behind her dressing screen to change. "I don't think I have a second pair for you though."

Annabeth snorted. "It's really sweet that you think digging could ruin my dress."

Sammy peeked over the screen. "I'll have you know I like that dress. The blue brings out your eyes. But that's okay. You can let me do the dirty work."

It was such a ridiculous statement, such a flip of the usual script, that Annabeth could only shake her head and chuckle.

A minute later, Sammy emerged, still tucking the blouse into the old trousers that she somehow made look chic and fashionable instead of ridiculous. She sat beside Annabeth again to put the boots on then stood with a grin. "Sally forth! Tallyho! We'll stop at the toolshed on our way out for a shovel."

Annabeth trailed her friend from the bedroom. "And you don't think it'll look suspicious to carry a shovel through town?"

"Hmm. A good point. How about a garden trowel? That would be easier to conceal as we're walking. Did you see how deep he buried the box? Will that suffice?"

Though she'd played the memory over again and again in her mind, Annabeth still had to shrug. "I couldn't really tell. It didn't look terribly deep, but I wasn't that close and it was pretty well dark out. Honestly, I don't expect there's even anything still there. He would have moved it, wouldn't he? He knew I saw him."

"Maybe, maybe not. He might not have had time, especially after chasing you to town. We won't know until we see for ourselves."

Annabeth could have argued more, but she knew Sammy well enough to realize there'd be no point to it. She wouldn't be able to dissuade her friend, and frankly she didn't want to. Annabeth had been itching to see for herself if the box was still there and had been frustrated when she couldn't find an opportunity to investigate.

Besides, an outing with Sammy was bound to be fun, even if the reason wasn't a happy one. She would have suggested they stop and recruit Pru, except that she didn't want to involve anyone else in this if she could help it.

The day was bright, the sunshine warm, even though the September air was cool. By an unspoken agreement, they chatted only of normal things after liberating a garden trowel from the shed and as they walked through town, lest anyone overhear them. They also avoided the busiest streets, given Sammy's unusual clothing.

Annabeth thought they'd made it all the way through town without incident—until an unexpected male voice brought them to a halt just as they passed the last buildings. "Miss Adams? Miss Billings? What brings the two of you out into the countryside like this?"

Sammy hissed out a breath and squeezed her eyes shut. For a moment, Annabeth thought she meant to ignore Reverend Cassidy altogether. But that wouldn't do, would it?

With an encouraging hand on her best friend's elbow, Annabeth pivoted to face him. He must have been paying a visit to the Parsons' farm, judging by the path he was on, which made sense. Mrs. Parsons had been down with pneumonia for two weeks now. Annabeth pasted a smile onto her face. "Afternoon, Reverend. We're reliving some of our childhood adventures."

Sammy had also turned, and now she linked their arms together and gave him a smile so bright it surely blinded him. "That's right. You weren't around then, but Annie and I used to run all over the place seeking adventure. We thought it a fine day to reclaim a bit of it." As if in proof, she made a show of dragging in a deep breath and letting it out with a satisfied sound. "I adore autumn. Don't you?"

Benjamin Cassidy looked like what he adored was a young woman so determined to enjoy a pretty day. A grin played over his lips as he nodded. "Indeed. There is little I enjoy more than being out in God's beautiful world. Though you now have me quite curious. What trouble did the two of you used to stir up?" Amusement glinted in his eyes as he looked from one of them to the other.

Annabeth bit her lip. They had plenty of stories they could trot out—but Sammy might smack her if she dared share some of them.

Her friend laughed. "Oh, no. If we tell you, you'll lose all respect for us. We were utter rapscallions, weren't we, Annie?"

"If our mothers had known the half of it, they would have forbidden us from ever leaving our houses." Or at least, they would have pretended to be horrified. She suspected that Bess Adams had found her fair share of trouble as a girl too, and Mother had many a story about sneaking out of the school for the deaf she'd attended as a child.

The reverend grinned. "I hope someday you'll deign to share a few of those stories. At the moment, however, you're off the hook. I'm late for my next appointment." He tipped his hat and stepped onto the road. "I pray you have a lovely afternoon, ladies. And if you find any trouble today, you can be assured I'll keep my lips buttoned about seeing you out here."

They laughed, but Annabeth suspected she wasn't the only one whose heart was hammering. Though Sammy's was likely doing so for reasons other than nearly getting caught before they even started digging. Her friend sighed and watched the reverend walk away.

They continued walking as soon as he was out of view, and when Annabeth pointed to the trees she'd taken cover in that night, they checked to make sure no one was looking before darting into the foliage.

"This is where I was standing." Annabeth tugged Sammy to a halt and pointed to the field on the other side of the trees. "And that's where he was. Beneath that oak, there at the corner of the field." The field was blessedly empty of workers, unlike every other time Annabeth had walked by.

Sammy nodded. "Okay. Let's go."

Annabeth led the way to where Edwin had been digging, as best she could tell. Sure enough, there was a patch at the base of the oak tree where the grass had clearly been dug up and then put back.

Brandishing her garden trowel, Sammy fell to her knees and began digging. Annabeth knelt beside her, lifting the chunk of sod out of the way then watching for any telltale glint of metal.

Several minutes later, Sammy had perspiration glinting on her brow, but they'd uncovered nothing but a couple of rocks.

Annabeth sat back with a huff. "He's moved it. It couldn't have been deeper than this."

That was smart of him, of course, but still frustrating. It made her glad she hadn't gone to the police. If she had, she'd have made a laughingstock of herself.

She'd have dragged them out to this field only to dig up the disturbed earth and find nothing.

Not that she'd seriously considered approaching law enforcement, not without solid proof in hand. And even then, what were the chances that anyone would believe her—the invisible daughter of two pariahs who had barely two pennies to rub together—over Edwin Buchanan? If she pointed a finger at him, he'd only have to laugh and deny it, and those charges would come right back around on her. She would be accused of being the one who had stolen whatever was in that box.

She knew it was true. It had happened to her father. And though there hadn't been enough evidence to arrest him, it had added to the stories people told about him. One more reason they claimed as to why they didn't trust him. He was a criminal, just one too crafty to be caught.

What wretched lies, and yet people were so eager to believe them.

Well, she wouldn't give them the chance to tell such lies about her. She couldn't control what others made up, but she could avoid giving them an opening.

Sammy sat back too. "We can keep searching."

"But where? The countryside is so vast, and we can't check every inch." She shook her head, clasping her hands together when they threatened to tremble. "I don't see any other ground here that seems to have been disturbed. And where else would we even check?

Closer to the Buchanan house? We don't dare go poking around their property. We'd get caught."

Reaching up to massage her temples, Sammy said, "We can't go to the police without proof. It would be our word against Edwin's."

Annabeth leaned over and wrapped Sammy in a hug. "*We* aren't doing anything. But I love you for saying it."

"If you think I'm letting you face this alone, you're crazy," her friend replied.

"I know I can count on you." She leaned back, hands still on Sammy's shoulders. "You've already helped, even without realizing it. And the fact that you'd come out here like this with me—that means the world."

Sammy's nostrils flared, then her lips pressed into a tight line. "You need to stay with me until things blow over. Bring the chickens if you want. It's not safe for you, all alone in that cabin in the middle of nowhere."

"He doesn't know where I live." All the proof she needed of that fact was that two weeks had gone by and he hadn't cornered her at home. "Even if someone tried to tell him, he wouldn't be able to find it. No one from town ever goes out there." Even Sammy would have a hard time following the trail through the woods, and she'd been to Annabeth's house a few times over the years.

It just wasn't the sort of place you invited your friends to visit. Not that Annabeth had been ashamed of her parents or what they'd provided for her, but every time Sammy had come, Mother had been so frazzled, trying to make their rickety old homestead presentable.

It had been easier on everyone for Annabeth to go to Sammy instead.

"I still don't like it. I don't like you being alone out there in general. How would anyone ever know if something happened to you? If you fell and broke your leg, you could die before help knew to come. But now, with someone *threatening* you? How do you expect me to sleep at night when my best friend is in that kind of danger?"

"He hasn't threatened me." But when Sammy glared at her, she gave it up. "All right, he's clearly been trying to corner me, but I'm sure it's simply to have a conversation. He probably wants to try to explain himself, sure I'll believe whatever he says because he's *Edwin Buchanan*."

"Or bribe you into keeping quiet." Sammy lifted her chin, eyes glinting. "Maybe you should let him. Assure him you *do* believe him, and that you'll stay quiet. Then this goes away."

"Have you never read a novel? It never just *goes away*. And I won't accept a bribe. It wouldn't be right."

Rather than call out her stubbornness, Sammy waved a hand in dismissal. "Of course not, but he doesn't know that, does he? All we need is for him to believe you're no threat to his secret. Then you keep your head down, and he gets lulled into a false sense of security."

"And I find that box wherever he buried it and gather my evidence and—" She sighed, shoulders slumping. "And nothing. No one would believe me."

Sammy lifted her chin. "Well, they'll believe *me*. Which is why we are going to find the truth of this together. And then, when you prove yourself a true heroine, everyone will have to look at you with the respect you deserve."

Annabeth's lips curved up of their own volition. It was too difficult not to smile at Sammy, even when she proposed the impossible. "If only the world were as simple as that."

Folding her dirty arms over her chest, Sammy scowled at her. "You always try to complicate things. And I say this with all the love in the world, but you always assume the worst about people."

Because she'd *seen* the worst of people, sides to them that Sammy never saw. Traits no one else seemed to see. Everyone in town seemed to believe that Glen MacGivens had simply happened to find Eloise Gray's lost necklace, that Gracie Ratchford hadn't meant to walk out of Fisher's Department Store with a bag full of sweaters she didn't pay for, or that Shirley Sanderson had given up smoking.

But she sealed her lips against saying any of those things to Sammy. Who was she to spill anyone's secrets or to ruin her best friend's rosy view of the world? She'd win no friends by blabbing. She'd slip it all into her story to add color and nuance and then change all the names so no one knew who she was talking about.

And if her little story was ever somehow published and someone happened to recognize themselves in the book, perhaps the mirror held up to them would inspire them to change.

Or, more likely, to hate Annabeth for her audacity and cling to that resentment instead of turning over a new leaf.

She summoned a smile for Sammy. "I know I seem pessimistic to you. And maybe you're right. Maybe people would respect me if I could outsmart Edwin."

"Of course they would." Sammy pushed to her feet. "Let's go back to the house. We need to make a plan."

Annabeth laughed, even as exhaustion rolled through her. She'd gotten up at the crack of dawn to take care of her own chores before heading into town to clean her Saturday morning houses and then had walked to Sammy's. Now her arms and legs were doing a good imitation of rubber. Or lead. Or some strange combination of both—the bend of rubber and the weight of lead. "Maybe tomorrow, after church. I'd like to get home early enough to get some writing in tonight."

It was the one thing that always made Sammy relent. She brushed off the trowel and slid it back into her pocket. "Oh, all right. But by the time you come back tomorrow, I'll have a full plan ready to be launched, make no mistake."

Another laugh bubbled up. "I don't doubt it." She moved over to give her friend another hug. "Thank you."

"For what?"

"Being you." One more squeeze, then Annabeth turned toward the trees. "Want me to walk you home?"

"And then have to backtrack? No, I'll be fine. We're barely outside of town." They moved together into the trees, pausing when they emerged once more and the road stretched out before them.

Sammy reached for Annabeth's hand and gave her fingers a squeeze. "Be careful, Annie." Her tone was serious, heavy.

Annabeth nodded. "I will be. It's still daylight. I'll be fine."

Sammy didn't look appeased. "I wish you had a telephone so you could let me know when you get home."

Talk about wishful thinking. Most of the houses in town had telephones, but the lines hadn't been strung all the way out to where she lived. "I'll be fine, like I always am."

Sammy sighed. "I'll have to entrust you to the Lord. An exercise in faith."

"Spoken like a future pastor's wife." Annabeth winked and turned away from town.

Laughter followed her as Sammy turned the opposite way. "I'll see you tomorrow."

Annabeth called a farewell over her shoulder and hurried toward Sweet Hollow Road. Her fingers positively itched for her typewriter. Though she might never discover where Edwin had put that box he'd been burying, nor what was in it, she'd already woven the plot into her novel. In *Blackberry Secrets*, a large portion of the Buchanan fortune had been stolen and buried under that oak tree. It was just what she'd needed to make the story come together.

Because the schoolmarm, boarding in the Buchanan house as she was, saw the thief. That was why she'd been murdered.

It made for a wonderful murder mystery, but turning her real situation into one might also be why she'd been jumping at every shadow. No matter how many times she told herself that Edwin wasn't likely to resort to murder, her fictitious villain had done exactly that. And those were the thoughts she went to sleep with every night.

Still, the story was coming quickly now. And it wasn't merely exciting to see it shaping up. It was downright therapeutic. She could write out every injustice she saw, and then she could soften it as she imagined her mother's kind replies. Her reminders that people were never only what was visible. There was a world of hurt and hope underneath.

Hannah Jane Prentiss, for example. Since her comment about the cookies, she'd been almost soft. Well, no, not soft. But gentler somehow. She'd sent a jar of soup home with Annabeth last week, for no reason at all. She'd even smiled when she said, "Bring the jar back when you're done."

Mother was right. People were more than just their worst parts. Annabeth knew it, though she rarely saw evidence of it in most of them. But little things like that reminded her it was true. It made her determined to make her Hannah Jane character deeper, richer than she'd first intended.

After walking half a mile on the road, she left it in favor of a deer trail behind the blackberry brambles, the same path she always took. It was scarcely visible from the road, so she checked to make sure no one was watching and ducked behind the briars. Within seconds, she'd be as invisible to any passersby as the trail itself.

A few birds took wing as she passed beneath them, squirrels chattering on the branches and racing up the tree trunks. All the tension from the day eased from her shoulders as she ducked under a low-hanging hickory limb and walked through leaf-green light toward the sanctuary of home.

The cabin came into view, its ancient logs so moss-covered that it might as well have sprouted from the forest floor. Only the tin roof looked out of place, though it was rusty enough that it didn't glint in the sunlight anymore to give it away. The rust had eaten all the way through in two spots, and she'd done her best to patch it. One of these days, she'd have to replace it altogether. Somehow.

Then, the unthinkable happened. Someone stepped out from behind the far side of the cabin. Someone tallish, trim, and dressed in clothes far too expensive for this place. Someone with dark hair, deceptive blue eyes, and an expression that couldn't be as innocently beseeching as it appeared.

Edwin Buchanan took another step with his hands lifted, as if in surrender. "Miss Billings—please. Don't run."

Chapter Thirteen

The library's interior was cool and quiet, making Hannah aware of how hot the sun had been on her shoulders outside. She glanced around the familiar entryway, trying to see it from the eyes of a stranger.

What would have caught a journalist's attention in here? Why had a reporter come to the local library, where presumably she couldn't check anything out if she wasn't from the area? She'd be relegated to what she could read while visiting.

But there were things the journalist might discover *only* in the local library, specifically in the historical society room. Hannah headed in that direction, a bit surprised when she saw Alice Tyler at the case with a new display every month—not just looking at it, but working on it.

Hannah approached, her curiosity increasing by the second. "Morning, Alice," she said quietly as she came up, looking from Alice to the picture frame in her hand. It was a black-and-white photo of a thirtysomething-year-old woman in 1940s-style clothing, with her hair in victory rolls. "Oh, who's that?"

Alice greeted her with a small smile and set the photo on the shelf. "Prudence Tyler Grant—my late husband's aunt."

"Ah, the Pru Tyler from the novel?"

It must have been the wrong thing to say, because Alice's features clouded over. Hannah couldn't think why. The author had nothing but good things to say about Pru, and the other Tylers were scarcely mentioned at all.

"If you can call three lines enough to say she was even *in* the book. Of all the families to underrepresent. The Tylers were pillars of this town back then. It's criminal how this Smith person ignored them so fully."

"Wait." Hannah examined the shelves. The entire display seemed to be about the Tylers, given the notecards accompanying each photo. "You're upset because your family doesn't appear *more* in the book?"

"My husband's family." Alice frowned at Hannah's failure to understand. She felt a little silly. Alice had already mentioned that Pru was her late husband's relative, not her own. "I don't even know my own family. I was abandoned as a child in Lexington and grew up in a home for orphans. But when I met Stan in college and he brought me home, his family took me in like I was one of their own. They were the best people I've ever known, every one of them. They ought to have been the heroes of that book." She pulled another frame from a box at her feet and positioned it beside the photo of Pru.

For a moment, Hannah just stood there. She'd had no idea that Alice had such a rough start to life, nor that she hadn't moved to Blackberry Valley until she'd married Stan Tyler.

But one thing was clear—Alice had nothing to do with the writing of *Blackberry Secrets*, or she wouldn't be so upset about the Tylers' lack of page-time.

Clearing her throat, Hannah faced the display case. "So, what are you doing with this?"

"Giving the Tyler family the honor they deserve." She pulled out a handful of boxes and opened them, revealing military medals. "These belonged to Stan's grandfather. He gave his life at Normandy in World War II, you know. Stan's father was only a baby when he signed up."

"I imagine they missed him so much, but were proud of him."

Hannah reached for another photo, this one also featuring Pru, but with her arms around two other young women Hannah didn't recognize. One was blond, with a striking face and a beautiful smile as she laughed. The other's smile was a little more restrained, her features more delicate and hair a darker shade, though there was no telling what color it was in the black-and-white photo. It could have been any shade of brown or red.

"Do you know who these women are with Pru?" Hannah asked.

"Pru's mother always wrote on the backs of photos everyone's names, ages, and the dates they were taken. This here is Samantha Adams," Alice said, indicating the blond. "Her family owned the mansion outside of town that's maintained by the historical society now. They do all those tours and whatnot. And this is Annabeth Billings. She grew up poor but ended up marrying into a good family, I think. The three were always good friends, all their lives. We have photos of them together, starting as children and going up into their eighties."

Hannah smiled. "Lifelong friends. I love that." Her gaze lingered on Alice's face. *Annabeth Billings...She grew up poor...* Who, perhaps, had worked as a housecleaner to make ends meet? Her scalp prickled at the possibility that she had finally found the person she was looking for. "Do you know, by chance, if Annabeth ever went by Annie?"

"As a child she did, yes." Alice handed her a smaller snapshot of the same three girls, but no more than ten years old. "This one says 'Pru, Sammy, and Annie' on the back. Why?"

"I think my great-grandmother mentioned her in an old diary entry." Hannah studied the childhood photo, not sure whether to smile at the camaraderie of the trio or sigh sadly at the threadbare state of Annie's dress. She was barefoot in the photo, while the other two girls wore patent-leather Mary Janes.

Hannah committed the name Annabeth Billings to memory, certain the woman had something to do with *Blackberry Secrets*. It was the only explanation for how things she'd witnessed ended up in the book.

Hannah cleared her throat. "Did you by chance talk to the woman who left the library right before I came in? The blond, smartly dressed?"

Alice gave her another look that questioned her astuteness. "You mean Hailey Cassidy?" She made a clicking sound with her tongue. "You young people don't even bother watching the news anymore, do you?"

"I do, actually. I just couldn't recall her last name." She set the photo on the shelf. "I was surprised to see her in Blackberry Valley. Is she covering a story here or something?"

Alice shrugged. "She didn't volunteer much. Just said she was doing some research and asked if I knew what display had been up before this one. I told her to ask Phyllis Taft."

Alice had clearly not been starstruck by a local celebrity. But it also didn't sound like Hailey Cassidy was on the same trail that Hannah was following. Which might mean that Hannah had a chance to find answers before they were plastered on the morning news—or, it might mean she was on the wrong track altogether.

Time would tell.

Hannah blinked as she stepped out of the church doors and into the bright sunlight, smiling when she saw Liam standing on the sidewalk, his phone in hand. She'd scrolled through social media last night for an update on the training fire but hadn't seen one. She hoped that wasn't a bad sign. That plume of black smoke had lasted a lot longer than she'd expected yesterday.

"Hey," she said in greeting as she approached him. "How did it go yesterday? Did you make it to the festival last night?"

Liam slid his phone into his pocket and angled a tired smile her way. "It took a little longer than I'd hoped. Not too bad, but I was so tired by the time we wrapped up that I asked Gramps if he'd be okay with us going tonight instead. He was gracious enough to reschedule the game night he had planned with a few of his friends to accommodate."

For a moment, she almost hoped that a small part of his reschedule had been because he knew she'd be there tonight. Though that was silly. Maybe sometimes she thought there was a spark between them, but neither of them had time for dating right now. Clearly. She'd been neglecting the people already in her life. How would she carve out time for someone else? "Glad that worked out. You'll probably be able to enjoy it more this way, though I guess now I can't ask you for recommendations on which stalls I should watch for."

"I'm afraid not. Though if you see Coop's Candy Apples, definitely check those out. Best caramel apple I ever had came from that stand last year." He looked past her and lifted a hand to someone in greeting. "Hey, guys. I hear you and Hannah are hitting up the festival today."

Hannah followed his gaze and found Lacy and Neil behind her. "Well, the girls are going. I'm going to stay home and work on my *fantasy* novel," Neil said with exaggerated emphasis, aimed at Hannah and topped with a wink.

She winced. And it was only a *little* exaggerated. "Sorry. Sorry."

Liam frowned in confusion. "I'm missing something."

Hannah sighed. "I let my imagination run away with me the other night and thought, 'Wow, Neil has old maps of Blackberry Valley and access to all this historical stuff and obviously loves books, so he could totally be B.B. Smith!' Completely ignoring the fact that my best friend would never keep such a thing from me."

"Nor could her husband ever hope to keep quiet about it if he landed a publishing deal," Neil added. To her relief, he seemed highly amused by the whole idea. "Honestly, I'm flattered you considered for even a moment that I could have written that book. Even if it's not a genre I ever see myself writing."

"In her defense, you do love reading it." Lacy moved to Hannah's side, her words warming Hannah from the inside out. A few days ago, she had condemned Hannah's silly question. But that was the great thing about a best friend. They forgave the stupid stuff and bumped their shoulder into yours to make it clear all was forgiven. "And after he finished laughing when I told him about it, he started thinking about all these historical resources you said we have and remembered that he'd seen some old boxes in the basement that might have stuff from the 1930s. We could look through it before we head to the fairgrounds, if you want."

Hannah knew a peace offering when she heard one. "That would be great, if you don't mind the delay."

"Not at all. I'm too hungry to wait until we get there to eat anyway, so we can grab a sandwich at the farm and go through some of the stuff. We'll have plenty of time at the festival."

Hannah nodded her approval of the plan. "Great. Liam and his grandfather are going this afternoon too."

Liam smiled and shifted away. "Maybe we'll see you ladies there. I have a couple things to take care of before I go pick up Gramps, so I need to get going for now."

They said their farewells, and after a quick exchange to agree that Hannah would drive herself to the farm and they'd decide from there which of them was driving to the fairgrounds, they too were on their way to the parking lot and their respective vehicles.

Once at the farm, Hannah changed from her church clothes into the shorts and top she'd brought to wear to the festival. By the time she got out of the bathroom, Lacy already had three sandwiches made, and Neil was tromping up the basement stairs with a few old cardboard boxes in his arms.

"One more trip ought to do it," he said as he put the boxes down beside a few others. "Not sure if any of these are from the right era, but we'll see."

Hannah shook her head. "Man, people's attics and basements are real treasure troves, aren't they?"

"Of junk someone couldn't bear to part with that later generations don't know enough about to know if they should toss it or not?" Lacy laughed and toed one of the boxes. "I peeked in one of these once. I literally found fifty years' worth of Christmas cards that my grandparents had kept from everyone under the sun. All signed with things like 'Carol and Joe,' as if I have a clue who those people are."

"I bet just seeing how the designs of the cards have changed or not was fascinating though." Hannah crouched down to sift through one of the boxes.

Lacy laughed. "You are such a sentimentalist sometimes. And you sound like Neil."

"What?" Neil called from the stairs. "Did she say something brilliant?"

"No, something cheesy." Lacy moved to close the basement door behind him after he emerged with the last box. "Let's eat before we dive into this. Those things are dusty, and I'd just as soon not eat all the dirt from the basement."

"You are a wise, wise woman." Hannah abandoned the box she'd been poking through and moved to the sink to wash her hands. "I wonder if there are any cards from Annabeth Billings to whomever would have been around in the 1930s. Maybe something that was left behind." She'd already called Lacy yesterday on her way back to the Hot Spot to tell her about the Annie/Annabeth connection.

"From what I can tell, everyone in Blackberry Valley used to send Christmas cards to everyone else, so probably." Lacy moved the plates of sandwiches to the table and set a bag of chips between them. "Honey, you want to get the hummus and carrots from the fridge?"

Given that the person she likely meant as "honey" was en route to the sink to wash his hands, Hannah said, "I'll get them." She was at the farm enough not to feel at all odd digging through her friend's crisper drawer for the carrots or moving things around on the shelf in search of hummus.

Once they were all seated, Neil said grace and they dug in.

"What are you thinking you might learn from the cards?" Lacy asked as they ate, her gaze fixed on Hannah.

Hannah shrugged. "I don't know. Any new information, I guess. Alice said she married someone from town, which is no doubt the last name she ended up using, as well as the one her kids would have. If I knew that, I could probably figure out who her modern descendants are."

"Sounds simple enough." Neil shook some chips from the bag onto his plate.

"Assuming I'm even right, that this is the Annie from the stories. And that she's the one who wrote all these things down and left them to her family."

"It makes sense. The way I see it, only two people knew about that cookie jar exchange, right?" Lacy said. "Hannah Jane and Annie. And I don't think it's the kind of story either of them would have told other people. Even if the Hannah Jane version is available online now, that's a pretty recent endeavor, isn't it? When did Maeve get that website up?"

"Maybe a year or so ago," Hannah said.

Neil tilted his head as he munched. "I'm no expert, of course, but from what I've read in the online groups I've joined, most publishers are working one to two years out, which means this book has been in the editorial process for at least a year, maybe more. And it's pretty unlikely that someone's debut novel was whipped out in a few short weeks and then picked up overnight by such a big publisher. Not to say it couldn't have happened, but most writers take a while to work on a book, and then it can take quite a long time to find a publisher."

Hannah dipped a baby carrot in the hummus she'd spooned onto her plate. "So, while it's possible that someone saw Maeve's site a year ago and added those historical details to a book that was already in the editorial process, it might be more likely that they had the story longer. Which would mean they didn't get it from Hannah Jane's journals, but from something that Annie recorded."

"I'll have to find time to go to the library tomorrow." Lacy crunched a chip. "I want to see what this Annabeth looked like. Anyone you know bear a resemblance, Hannah?"

"Not that struck me. Though I only saw photos from when the women were our age and younger. If Alice brought newer ones, she didn't have them out yet while I was there." She took a bite of her ham and cheese, mulling it over. She tried to remember Annabeth's delicate features and pair them up with more familiar faces. She set her sandwich down as a new idea struck. "What if it's Hailey Cassidy? What if she isn't here to break the story, but because she wrote it? She could be hanging around to see what the reaction is."

Lacy paused with her sandwich halfway to her mouth. "Do Hailey and Annabeth look alike?"

Did they? "Not really. Hailey has bigger eyes and defined cheekbones, and her hair is way lighter than Annabeth's."

"Hailey could have dyed her hair," Neil said.

"That's a fair point," Lacy mused. "Seems like a lot of the female news anchors favor that hair color, and I have a suspicion they don't all come by it naturally." She winked at Hannah. "Clearly they just want to look more like you."

Hannah batted her lashes and gave her light, shoulder-length locks a toss. "Clearly. Regardless, Hailey *could* still be related. After all, I don't think I resemble Hannah Jane even though she's my relative."

"True. Not as much fun, but true." Lacy sighed as she moved her gaze to the boxes. "What are the chances the answer is actually waiting in the stuff from our basement?"

Hannah shrugged. "We won't know until we look."

They each grabbed a box and made themselves comfortable. Hannah ended up with the one full of Christmas cards, which really was fascinating from an artistic point of view. As she flipped them open and closed again, the names began to grow familiar, though none of them seemed particularly relevant. She didn't see any signed *Annie* or *Annabeth*.

But then, many of them just had last names. *Merry Christmas from the Jacksons* or *the Buchanans* or *the Millers*.

By the time she got to the bottom of the box, she hadn't learned anything new. "Well, that was no help."

"Nothing from Annie?"

"She could have been included with one of the family names, but I have no way to tell. There was no Billings, but until I know her married name, she could be behind any of these other cards, or none of them."

"There has to be a way to find out. Marriage records or something," Neil said from beside a pile of...ashtrays?

She burst out laughing. "Wow. That is quite a collection."

Neil lifted up a particularly creative one in mustard yellow. "I didn't know anyone here smoked."

"Now, now. Maybe my family considered them sculptures. Fine art." Lacy dumped an armful of stuff in her box. "Where would we go to find marriage records? The church? Courthouse?"

Hannah grabbed her phone from the table where she'd left it. "Or, we ask someone who's already set up for all this research."

Grinning, she scrolled through her contacts for John Comstock.

Chapter Fourteen

Blackberry Valley,
April 25, 1936

Edwin Buchanan took a slow step closer, hands still raised. "Please. I mean you no harm."

Annabeth wasn't fool enough to believe him. But he'd found her *here*, where she'd thought she'd always be safe.

She slid back to maintain their distance, but she knew there was no point in running. Where could she go? Nowhere in town was safe from him, and even if she could outpace him on the forest trails, he'd only corner her somewhere else, some other time. Leaving town wasn't an option—she had no funds to get herself away and nowhere to go.

And if he was willing to hunt her down here, would even the Adamses' house be safe from him? He could knock on the door and ask to see her, and Sammy's parents would show her into the drawing room where he waited, oblivious to any reason not to.

No. If he'd found her here, he could find her anywhere else. It was time to stop running. Stop hiding. Time to change tactics. She'd hear him out, make him think she agreed with whatever he said. Let him think, as Sammy had said, that he'd bought her off and she was no threat to him.

The best way to play that role would be to cower, to act timid.

She couldn't bring herself to do it. Her chin came up of its own volition, and she crossed her arms over her chest. And why not? Perhaps if he had to work for her supposed capitulation, he'd be more apt to believe it. "You have some nerve, showing up here uninvited. You're lucky I don't have my daddy's shotgun on me."

For some inexplicable reason, he smiled, though his hands stayed up. "An answer to my frantic prayers, perhaps. Can we talk? Just for a minute. I need to explain what you saw that night."

If he thought she was going to invite him inside, he was in for a surprise. She didn't budge, not even to motion a silent invitation to sit on one of the stumps Daddy had shaped into rough chairs and stationed by their door. She could imagine Mother having something to say about her rudeness, but Annabeth was trying to feel in control of the situation. "Have your say."

His arms sank a bit, but somehow it didn't look like it was because he felt any ease. It was more as if his whole self had sagged with a burden. "I realize it must have been suspicious, seeing me digging a hole at night and burying a moneybox."

So it *had* been money. "'Suspicious' is a fine choice of words."

His nod seemed heavy, sorrowful. "My father asked me to, while he and Mother were out for the evening. It was our own money I was burying—everything that had been in the safe at home."

A strange sort of tightness began in her chest, the kind usually inspired by one of Mother's challenging looks, by the signs she'd make to tell Annabeth she was judging too harshly, that she needed to go deeper and find her compassion and understanding.

But his words made little sense. "Why in the world would your father ask you to bury your own money?" She hadn't seen inside the safe that day she was caught in Mr. Buchanan's office, but she'd seen the stack of cash he'd carried as he walked toward it. If he put a stack that big in there every week, the moneybox Edwin had hidden would contain a hefty amount. Though that didn't explain much.

Edwin's sigh seemed to drain the last of his strength. His arms drooped back to his sides, though he lifted one hand again to rub his face. "I will tell you the truth, but I have to summon the audacity to beg for your discretion. For my mother's sake."

He didn't sound like a man trying to get away with a crime. He sounded like someone trying to stand upright after a horrible blow. She moistened her lips. "Your mother?"

"She has a problem. Gambling. It's why we had to leave Louisville. The races, you see—she nearly bankrupted us ten years ago. My sister's due to have a baby in a few weeks, and Mother is going to be with her. That's as it should be, but it means she'll be there during the Kentucky Derby. She's taken money from the safe before. Father has changed the combination, but she always cracks it eventually, and then money goes missing."

Now Annabeth sank onto one of the chairs Daddy had made. Mrs. Buchanan had a gambling problem serious enough that her husband had to hide their money from her? For all her tendency to see the worst in people as Sammy accused, Annabeth never would have guessed that the elegant Buchanan matriarch was hiding such a secret.

Knowing it, however, resulted in more questions rather than answers. A dozen of them rattled around in her mind, but she started with what seemed like the simplest and most obvious. "Why doesn't your father put the money in the bank?"

Edwin shook his head. "After the crash? He doesn't trust them. And besides, in a town this size, even if her name isn't on the account, she could go in and ask for a withdrawal and the teller would give it to her."

Annabeth's breath came out in a slow gush, and with it went all the preconceived notions she had about the Buchanan family. Mrs. Buchanan wasn't just a socialite with no worries beyond seeing that her children made good matches. Mr. Buchanan wasn't merely a businessman concerned with making a profit. And Edwin wasn't some spoiled heir who only spoke to her to irritate his mother. They were a family with problems, different from hers, but no less serious. A family trying to manage as best they could when they must feel at loose ends.

Money had always been a problem for her family, but she'd never imagined it could be such a different kind of problem for people like the Buchanans. She'd always thought that if one *had* money, that would erase all money-related problems.

How wrong she'd been.

"I'm sorry, Edwin. That's a lot for you and your father to have to deal with." But she didn't doubt him, not for a second. She knew a liar when she saw one, and Edwin's tone and features confirmed that he was telling the truth. A hard truth that he didn't *want* to tell.

He motioned toward the second chair, brows arched. When she nodded her permission, he sat, leaning forward to brace his elbows on his knees, his gaze on the leaf-littered ground rather than on her. "If we can keep her from getting the money in the safe before she leaves next week, it'll get us through the worst of it for a while. She'll likely put her hands on some at my sister's, but Cora knows Father will replace anything she takes. And Mother doesn't know where their safe is."

She would steal from her own daughter and son-in-law? The same woman who sat with her family in church every week, who donated to the food and clothing drives, who hadn't dismissed Annabeth when she was impertinent? It must be a terrible compulsion, one she was no doubt ashamed of.

And it impacted her whole family, was such a burden on them. Guilt pierced Annabeth when she realized she'd been adding to that burden these last two weeks every time she'd avoided Edwin. He must have been terrified that she would tell everyone what she'd seen him doing, and he'd have to race to offer an excuse—or else call her a liar.

Clearly, he and his father didn't want everyone to know about Mrs. Buchanan's problem. She couldn't blame them for that.

"I'm sorry I didn't give you a chance to explain earlier," she whispered.

He glanced over at her, that soft smile playing at the corners of his mouth again. "I hardly blame you. I could only guess what you thought, but none of the options would have been good. Were I in your shoes, I'd have cast me as a villain too."

Annabeth winced then let her own smile bloom as she thought about the novel underway on the other side of the wall at their back. "I might have done just that." It was good to know her imaginings had been pure fiction, but she still liked the fiction it had created. Especially now when she realized that the real man was far from a villain. He was simply a son trying to honor his mother and father in circumstances that made it rather tricky.

"Understandable. But I'm grateful you didn't report what you saw to the police. I'd have told them the truth, but I'm sure you understand why I'd rather not have to do that. I hate to besmirch my mother's reputation. She's a good woman, truly. She can't help this, somehow. She tries, but it's occasionally stronger than her will."

Heaven knew Annabeth had seen plenty of examples of that. "I didn't see the point—in going to the police, I mean. You could have denied it, and no one would have believed me over you."

At that, Edwin frowned. "Why would you say such a thing? Though, again, I wouldn't have denied it. It's one thing to try to protect my mother, but it's quite another to lie to the authorities."

How could a man like him, raised with the finer things of life, not understand? She motioned toward the cabin behind them, which was more like a shack. "You really have to ask? I'm poor. You're rich."

The way he looked at her then—no one had ever looked at her like that. He seemed genuinely baffled by her words. Like he didn't see *poor* when he glanced her way, but something more. "You're a hardworking, faithful young woman. You meet every harsh word with a kind one. You give respect to everyone, even when they don't deserve it. You shut down gossip when you could fuel it if you chose. You give to others even when you have little to spare. I can think of no qualities that would make anyone more reputable, and I daresay the authorities would agree."

She wasn't so sure, but she was too flabbergasted by the rest of what he'd said to focus on that. Obviously, he'd seen her work, but how would he know the other things? And he shamed her, too, with his praise. Enough that it made her cheeks go hot. "I may be respectful aloud, but you don't hear the things I say inside."

Instead of looking disappointed, he laughed. "And that only convinces me even more that I'd like to know you better. We all think things that aren't kind, Miss Billings. Learning when to button our lips against them is one of the most important lessons any of us ever learn, I think. A lesson many never seem to."

Did he really just say he wanted to know her better? The flush had no hope of fading now. "You give me too much credit."

"I don't think so. And I'm not saying that in the hopes that flattery will buy your silence. I hope you know that."

Given the blush creeping up *his* neck, she couldn't doubt he meant it. Even if she didn't know why. She ducked her head and cleared her throat. "I won't say anything. About your mother, I mean. The money. Well, except to Sammy—Samantha Adams. I'll have to tell her, because she already knows what I saw and is assuming the worst. I would like to tell her the truth to assuage her fears and clear your name with her. She won't say anything. You have my word on that. Sammy is the soul of discretion."

He frowned, clearly not happy that someone else needed to know, but after a long hesitation, he nodded. "I trust you."

He had no reason to, not really. But somehow, knowing that he did—well, that changed things. "I won't let you down."

Chapter Fifteen

"You know what would be convenient?" Lacy steered her truck into a field with a giant EVENT PARKING sign and followed the directions of a vest-wearing attendant down a bumpy row of parked vehicles, toward the spots still open at the end. "If Annie had married a Smith to match the author's last name. I'm sure there are Smiths in town. There are Smiths *everywhere*."

Hannah chuckled and grabbed the crossbody bag she'd brought for the outing. "I think if there was a Smith in town with the qualifications necessary to write a bestselling novel, it wouldn't be a secret anymore."

"Yeah, but the writer wouldn't have to *be* a Smith to be from a family with Smith on a branch of the tree. It would still be a logical place to start if John doesn't have any leads for us." Lacy parked and switched off the engine. "It would make sense for the writer to choose a pen name that was still a family name, wouldn't it?"

"It would." And it wasn't as if she'd already checked it out and found it to be a dead end. It just sounded so obvious once Lacy said it that she was certain *someone* had done it already. "Definitely worth digging into. Later. I've been informed by my very wise and loving best friend that I'm supposed to do nothing but have fun this afternoon."

Grinning, Lacy reached to grab her own purse from the back seat. "This friend sounds wise indeed. Let's go buy all the apple stuff."

It had been long enough since Hannah had attended a local festival as a guest that she didn't honestly know what to expect. As they walked toward rows of awnings and event tents, the scents and music that met them convinced her that Liam hadn't been wrong to recommend this. "Oh, man, something smells delicious. Why did you make us eat at home before we left, like reasonable adults?"

"Because I was starving, but we can totally stuff ourselves here too. We'll walk it off."

Hannah was pretty sure that the last time she'd been to the fairgrounds was when she'd gone to the county fair in high school. She almost expected to see carnival rides and food carts with flashing lights, well-lit games and award-winning livestock.

But this was a different sort of event. Booths with a variety of colored tents created rows and walkways through the open field. Horses walked in sedate circles at the end of the field with excited children on their backs. A three-legged race in an open area sparked laughter audible across the grounds, providing the perfect backdrop to a band playing on the grandstand.

The two friends couldn't see the concert from where they were, but they could hear it thanks to speakers set up throughout the field. She'd researched the festival yesterday and knew that several different groups were present. The one playing now would stop at three. It was a bluegrass group, and while that style of music wasn't Hannah's go-to genre, she knew talent when she heard it—and it made her feet want to walk and skip in rhythm.

She wasn't the only one. Lacy bopped along beside her. "Have you ever heard a sad banjo?"

"What?" Hannah laughed.

"Seriously. Listen to the lyrics, and they're pretty depressing. But it still sounds *happy*. Like something we should be dancing to. I'm convinced that a banjo cannot sound sad."

"You may be onto something there. I think you should buy their album and play it at your farm."

Lacy sent her a dubious look. "I should?"

"Hello—*Bluegrass* Hollow Farm. It's right there in your name. I bet Hennifer and Eggatha would love it. Doesn't music increase egg production?"

Lacy laughed. "I have no idea. But if I'm going to be playing it at my farm, then you need to start playing it in your restaurant. You know, because you serve Bluegrass eggs."

"I can't argue with that. After all, this band is local, so it fits the theme of the restaurant." Hannah grabbed Lacy's arm and pointed to one of the food tents. "Apple funnel cakes? I have never heard of those, but I am prepared to be educated."

"Oh, we are so trying those. Let's go."

They shared one—basically apple pie filling poured over a hot funnel cake, a combination Hannah decided she heartily approved of—while they browsed the nearby stalls, which offered far more than apple-themed merchandise. All sorts of people from the region had turned out to showcase their crafts and wares. There were tons of booths set up with activities for kids, artists of every sort, and food vendors galore.

Hannah had just spotted Coop's Candy Apples when Lacy grabbed her arm and spun her around, hissing, "No. Way."

Following her friend's pointing finger, Hannah soon learned what had elicited the response.

A white tent was set up behind the petting zoo, with a table full of books. But not just any books. *Blackberry Secrets*. And the banner hanging above it proclaimed, SIGNED BY THE AUTHOR!

No words were necessary. They both took off toward the tent, gazes seeking this author.

It couldn't be as simple as that, could it? The mysterious, anonymous B.B. Smith wouldn't simply be signing books at a local festival. Why bother with a pen name if they were going to show up at the county fairgrounds?

There was certainly no one sitting at a table with a pen in hand. The table held a few dwindling stacks of books. But a sixty-something woman sipping what looked like an iced coffee stood by another table with a cashbox and a little sign that cheerfully proclaimed they accepted credit cards.

Hannah went right up to the woman with a smile and asked outright, "Are you the author?"

The woman lowered her cup with a tired smile that said she'd heard that question about a thousand times already. "No, no. Just the bookseller." She pointed to another sign that said BARREN COUNTY BOOKS. "The author shipped me signed copies. Which means they can't be personalized, I'm afraid."

Hannah refused to be discouraged, latching on to the silver lining. "So you've communicated with the author? How did you reach out to them?" There was a website for B.B. Smith, but it didn't even have a contact form.

"B.B. reached out to me, actually." The woman pursed her lips. "Or maybe an assistant. I can't ever be sure." Obviously on a mission, she reached for a book. "Would you like one? Or maybe two?"

"Yes. Yes, we would," Lacy said, elbowing Hannah out of the way as if she knew Hannah had been about to say she already had a copy and didn't need another. "Two, please."

Though she didn't understand her friend's insistence, Hannah didn't object when Lacy handed over her card to pay for both copies at once. Even when her friend gave one of them to her as they left the tent.

They paused between two other booths, Lacy flipping the cover open. "Aha!"

"What?" Hannah opened her copy too, but it wasn't as though the scrawled signature revealed the author's real name. Frankly, she was only a little certain it was supposed to say B.B. Smith. It consisted mostly of two sloppy *B*s and a scribble that vaguely resembled an *S*. Or a *G*.

"I'm revising my theory on the gender of the author. This is absolutely a man's signature," Lacy said. "Tell me I'm wrong."

"Is that why you bought these? You could have just looked."

Lacy rolled her eyes. "You're kidding, right? If I went home without a couple signed copies when they were available, my husband would never forgive me."

Hannah laughed, well able to imagine that scenario. "Granted. But we probably should have come back for them. Now we have to carry them around all day."

"No problem." Lacy opened the flap of her bag, which was considerably larger than the one Hannah had chosen for the day, and slid her book inside. She held out a hand for Hannah's too. "Bookseller's wife here. I'm always prepared."

Hannah relinquished the second copy without complaint.

As they walked, she saw a lot of familiar faces from town, though plenty of unfamiliar ones too. She knew Drew and Allison had brought the kids the day before, and no doubt many of their neighbors and people from the other small towns in the county had come out for the festival too. It did make her wonder if B.B. Smith was from the area without being from Blackberry Valley itself. "Should I ask?" She glanced over at Lacy.

Lacy lifted her brows. "Ask what?"

Hannah motioned behind them, toward the book tent. "Why did B.B. contact *that* bookseller to run this booth instead of Neil, if he's all about the town where the book is set? Wouldn't the author want the Blackberry Valley bookstore to sell signed copies?"

"That is an excellent point." Lacy's face fell into a glower so exaggerated it was comical. "I think I'm mad now."

Hannah laughed and bumped her friend's arm. "Sorry. Not what I intended. And not what we're supposed to be focusing on today. I shouldn't have said anything."

Lacy's expression cleared, and she waved Hannah's comment away with a smile. "It's fine. Neil hates being stuck at events like this anyway. Probably for the best that B.B. didn't ask him."

They paused at a booth that sold watercolor paintings, where the artist was set up and creating new work while people watched. Hannah was always enthralled by people who made the visual arts appear so effortless. A dab here, a swipe there, and suddenly there was a tree or a horse or a mountain.

Lacy pointed to one of the finished works displayed on an easel. It was a landscape in spring colors, the Kentucky hills rolling into the distance under a breathtaking pastel sunrise. In the middle ground, a cluster of buildings nestled among the landscape, cozy and sleepy and half-shrouded in morning mist. "That would be gorgeous in your apartment. It matches your colors."

"It does." And Hannah still had some bare spots on the walls. Decorating hadn't exactly been a priority while she got a restaurant up and running. She moved over to the easel and checked the price. It was more expensive than a mass-produced print, but that made sense since it was an original. "That's not a bad price, right?"

"Not at all. I'd buy it if it matched my decor."

She studied it for another long moment. It could have been Blackberry Valley or any of the other small towns in the region. It felt like home. "I think I need it. I wonder if I can buy it and then pick it up on our way out."

"Or we can walk it back to the truck. We haven't come that far yet."

They ended up doing what Lacy suggested, depositing the signed books as well, and then reentering the festival through a different spot so they didn't cover the same ground twice. That was how Hannah spotted Liam and his grandfather at a booth that sold fresh apple cider by the glass or the gallon.

Hannah took a step toward them and stopped, glancing at Lacy. Her friend snorted. "Go ahead. You're allowed to say hello."

"But it's girls' night. Or day. Or whatever."

"Luckily, this girl is totally cool with being friendly with our neighbors. Especially the cute one you should totally go out with sometime."

"I don't know. I think Patrick might be a bit old for me," Hannah teased to escape the awkward conversation.

"That's not who I meant, and you know it." Lacy gave Hannah a nudge in the back. "Come on. Let's go say hi."

Patrick spotted them before Liam did, his face lighting up and arms going wide. "Hannah!"

"Hi, Mr. Berthold." She walked right into his embrace and gave him a hug. "So good to see you. How have you been?"

"Busy and having too much fun." He pulled back, still smiling. "How's the Hot Spot?"

"Also busy and having too much fun. You'll be pleased to know that we've been getting a lot of tourist traffic lately, and we've gotten a ton of comments about the memorabilia you provided."

"Excellent." He beamed at her friend. "Hey there, Lacy. How's the farm?"

Hannah and Lacy fell into step with the Berthold men as they moved away from the cider stall.

"Great. I never have to worry about eggs going unsold. There's this hot restaurant in town that always seems to need them," Lacy said with a grin.

"That's what I like to hear, for both of you. Did you see there's a news anchor from Louisville covering the event?" Patrick asked, tipping his chin to indicate something on the other side of the walkway.

They both turned, Hannah's eyes going wide when she saw the same blond woman from the bookstore and the library standing at a stall of corn-husk dolls, smiling and chatting with the woman and teen girl behind the table. "Hailey Cassidy is covering this event?"

"I assume so. She's here, isn't she?" Patrick scanned the area. "Though I don't see her cameraman anywhere. Do you see one, Liam?"

Liam made a cursory glance around, though surely they all would have noticed a camera crew. "No. Maybe she's here to enjoy the festival."

"She's entitled of course, but that would be a shame. I always like watching her. She's got sass but doesn't talk over her guests like some of them do, and she always presents things so they make sense. I'd like to hear what she has to say about the festival after all her years away."

"Years away?" Hannah snapped back around to face Liam's grandfather. "What do you mean? Is she from here?"

"Not Blackberry Valley specifically, but she grew up in the county. Didn't you know?" They meandered toward a booth selling caramel corn. Behind the tables of bagged popcorn, several people worked around a huge pot over a fire, stirring fresh kernels into caramel sauce. It smelled heavenly. "She's on lists about local celebrities or success stories from time to time. She was even on some big show out of New York for a couple years before she took the job in Louisville to be closer to her family."

There were a lot of things Hannah wasn't familiar with after her own years away. "I had no idea." She caught Lacy's gaze.

Hailey might not resemble Annabeth Billings, but they now knew she had local ties. Families moved among the small towns in the area all the time. Annabeth's children could have settled elsewhere in the county before Hailey was born. And the fact that she was still hanging around without a camera crew surely meant something, didn't it?

"I don't know," Lacy murmured, while Patrick and Liam bought a bag of caramel corn. "I still say that signature is a man's. But I suppose the sloppiness of the signature could be explained by unfamiliarity with signing a name that isn't the author's real one. And I guess we can't dismiss that she's here for a reason, and it doesn't seem to be visiting family. She's alone."

Hailey had been alone at the bookstore too. And at the library.

Hannah didn't know what it signified, exactly. But she had a feeling the woman wasn't there to cover the event.

Chapter Sixteen

Hannah and Lacy parted ways with Liam and his grandfather after about half an hour, when Patrick admitted that he'd like to get off his feet for a while. The two men headed toward the grandstand. Much as Hannah enjoyed browsing the lanes of stalls with them, she and Lacy weren't ready to sit quite yet. But they would meet up with the men later to watch the ceremony to name the winners of the apple pie contest—apparently a big deal with a substantial cash prize. Hannah wished she'd known about it beforehand so she could have entered.

"Okay, now we're free to trail her," Lacy whispered once the Bertholds were out of earshot, shooting a significant glance toward the shining blond head of Hailey Cassidy.

Hannah laughed. "Is that why you steered us this way? I thought you wanted to check out the apple seed mosaics."

"The what?" Lacy blinked at her and then at the unique artwork they'd stopped in front of. "Gracious, I didn't even notice those. They're interesting, but we're totally playing spy. Or sleuth. Whatever you want to call it. Try to look innocent, but we can't lose her."

Given that Hailey was meandering at a snail's pace toward the next booth, Hannah had to chuckle at her friend's urgency. She made a show of taking one step to the left. "There. Still in sight. Great sleuthing."

Reaching into her purse, Lacy put her back to Hailey then pulled out a mirror and used it to stare over her shoulder.

Hannah nearly choked on a laugh. "Lacy, seriously. I think you've had too much sugar."

"Shh. I'm trying to eavesdrop."

"On what? She's not saying anything." But it was fun to be playful like this. Hannah stepped around Lacy and into a tent full of crazy wigs and hats that she'd seen several kids sporting. "Do we need disguises?"

Lacy moved to her side, trying and failing to contain a giggle. "Oh my goodness. I so want to say yes, but I also don't want to spend money on these ridiculous things." She grabbed a wig with springy curls in red, orange, and yellow and held it over her head. "What do you think?"

"It's very you, as long as you top it off with one of these apple hats." Hannah reached for the plush apple design she'd seen a few people wearing, the things towering a foot high off their heads.

Lacy returned the wig to its stand but reached for a knitted red apple beanie, with a stem and leaf poking up from the crown. "This is actually adorable. I would wear this. I mean, not today because it's way too hot, but wouldn't this be cute at a farmers market when the weather cools?"

"It would be." Hannah reached for a knitted pumpkin hat clearly meant for a baby or toddler. "I think Allison had one of these for Ava. I distinctly remember photos so cute I had to show my friends at work. Think we could get Axel into one of these now?"

Lacy laughed at the thought of her rambunctious five-year-old nephew deigning to wear such a thing. "You should try. I mean, if you don't want to be the cool aunt anymore." She moved toward the vendor with the apple hat, digging in her purse for her wallet.

Hannah put the pumpkin back and peeked toward the booths opposite. "Better hurry," she stage-whispered to Lacy. "Our quarry is moving on."

Hailey had wandered to a booth whose vendor must have been a fan. The middle-aged crafter was reaching across the table to shake the anchor's hand, beaming as if her day had just been made. Curious as to how Hailey would respond, Hannah positioned herself behind a tent pole to watch.

In California, she'd seen a wide variety of celebrities. There were those who genuinely loved interacting with fans, and they made it clear in their enthusiasm. There were those who were gracious even when they clearly wanted to go about their day. Still others would begrudgingly take photos or sign napkins, making it clear that they were doing the fan an enormous favor. And there were those who would snap at fans and push by.

Hailey planted her flag in the first camp. She was beaming back at the woman, shaking her hand and holding it for a moment afterward between both of hers, saying something with animation and clear delight.

It was possible they actually knew each other. If Hailey had grown up in the area, then she'd have former teachers and old neighbors who remembered her. This could be a reunion instead of an introduction, but even so, it made Hannah like her to see the polished reporter lean in for a selfie with the woman.

Lacy joined Hannah, tucking her new hat into her purse. "Maybe that should be our approach. We can go up to her and gush about being big fans and flatter her into admitting whether she wrote the book or not."

"I thought you'd decided B.B. was a guy?"

"Yeah, but if we started following all the guys here around and gushing over them, my husband might have something to say about it."

It felt good to laugh as much as she had that day. Lacy had been right as usual—Hannah had needed this. Time away from the restaurant, away from responsibilities and mind-boggling puzzles. Even if they were still ostensibly trying to solve the author mystery, Lacy had made it fun instead of serious. "I still think it's more likely she's trying to get the scoop on who *did* write it. But you never know. I've been surprised before."

Hailey visited with her fan a bit more, purchased a cute wooden pumpkin sign with WELCOME, FALL painted on it in a pretty script, then moved off again.

They'd reached the end of the row of tents, but rather than circle around to the next ones, Hailey wandered toward the game area.

"Shall we?" Lacy headed that way too, a smile already on her lips as she watched scores of squealing, running, laughing kids taking part in the games and activities. The three-legged race had been replaced by a hop ball race, in which all the balls were painted to look like apples. Several children were trying to master small stilts that would allow them to pick apples from a few trees. Others enjoyed blowing bubbles, using bubble liquid gathered in a small apple-shaped inflatable pool. Hannah was impressed by the face painter who applied lavish designs with a steady hand in the midst of the chaos.

Some of the activities were aimed at adults too. There was a strength-testing machine in which the weights were measured in bushels of apples, one of those games where the player threw a ball—an apple-shaped one, in this case—at a pyramid of bottles and tried to knock them down. Even a tent set up for an apple pie-eating contest, which had apparently taken place the day before.

Hailey seemed genuinely enthralled by it all. She paused at one game after another, clapping with the other onlookers when someone, adult or child, performed well. She cheered on the participants in the hop ball race.

When she turned toward a giant apple-bobbing tub, Hannah leaned close to Lacy. "Think she's going to bob for apples?"

The tub was the size of a small, low swimming pool, and she didn't see a single person around its edges that had remained completely dry. Hailey was dressed more simply than the other times Hannah had seen her, in denim shorts and a simple red top that was obviously made of expensive fabric. But even so, she couldn't quite imagine the woman sticking her head in a tub of water to grab an apple with her teeth.

"I have my doubts. But this seems to be a pretty popular game."

There were people ringing the entire tub, only a few spaces open around the circumference. The classic activity seemed to draw people from all ages and inspired a lot of laughter in onlookers, as the players lunged at apples floating by only to come up with wet faces and no fruit. "I don't think I have ever actually bobbed for apples. You?"

"Maybe once in grade school." Lacy fanned herself with her hand. "I think these people are doing it to cool off. It's hot out here. Wanna try?"

Hannah's first instinct was to say no. Which made her wonder *why* her default was to say no. When had she stopped wanting to do things because she might look silly or mess up her hair? Why did being an adult have to mean being serious all the time? Especially when she'd so enjoyed not being serious with Lacy during their investigation. "Maybe we should. But let's watch for a few minutes first."

"Good idea," Lacy said. "Scope it out. Come up with our game-winning strategy." She pointed at a little boy who was reaching in with his hands. "I think that's a winning approach."

"No way. Flag on the play. Where's the ref?" Hannah grinned as she watched the little boy's mother correct him and mime the proper way to do it.

She felt someone move into the space on her other side. "This is so much fun, isn't it?" A woman's voice, smooth as honey. "I don't think I've seen bobbing for apples since I was a kid."

Hannah barely kept her jaw from dropping open when she saw Hailey Cassidy. Had their amateur tailing been busted? But Hailey didn't seem upset. Maybe she just wanted someone to talk to. She'd clearly come here alone, and that wouldn't be nearly as much fun as joking her way through the festival with a friend.

Might as well at least pretend they were totally innocent. Hannah grinned. "I definitely did not come across any apple-bobbing when I was living in California. We're working up the nerve to try it here."

"I will if you will. I don't recall seeing it in New York when I was there either." Hailey held out a hand. "Hailey Cassidy."

Hannah shook. "Hannah Prentiss."

Lacy leaned in too. "Lacy Minyard."

Hailey was nodding. Her gaze settled on Hannah. "You own the Hot Spot, right? I need to stop in before I head back to Louisville on Wednesday. I've been hearing about your new cookie jar." She flashed a television-worthy smile. "Brilliant idea. I'm so impressed with how the town's leaning into this thing with the novel."

"Are you going to do a story about it?" Lacy was clearly not feeling bashful today.

Hailey tilted her head to the side, her hair falling in a golden curtain. "I'm certainly considering it, if I can find the right angle. I'm mostly here to visit my parents, but we drive each other crazy if I do nothing but hang around the house all day. So when I realized the book was causing such a sensation, I thought I'd spend some time in Blackberry Valley to see how it was being received."

It sounded truthful. And reasonable. Certainly not like she was hiding her own authorship—though people had been known to lie, especially to strangers. But Hannah certainly wasn't going to ask her outright if she had hidden motives. Instead she asked, "Are your parents here?"

Hailey motioned toward the grandstand. "My dad's the banjo player. My mom's on staff, so she's here somewhere. If you see a crazy person running around barking orders, that's her." She said it with a fond smile.

"Your dad's on banjo?" Lacy repeated. "We were just talking about how there's no such thing as a sad banjo. It's so *happy* sounding."

"It's also annoying," Hailey deadpanned. Then she added a self-deprecating smile. "At least when you're an angsty teen who lives with it. Gotta say, I enjoy it much more now than I did then. I think I threatened to run away at least a dozen times between the ages of eleven and seventeen if he didn't stop."

"All that annoying practice clearly paid off," Hannah said. "He's really good."

"Just don't ask him to do 'Dueling Banjos' with his buddy."

Lacy's brows arched. "He won't?"

"No, he will. Every time. Forever. And my mother will glare at you until you run away from her visual daggers. She has come to *hate* that song." Hailey laughed, but it broke off when heated voices from the apple tub cut in.

"Oh, come on. Keep your kid in his own place, Ericson. Cayden would have had that one if Mason hadn't knocked it away."

"Will you lighten up, Parker? It's how the game goes."

"Oh boy," Lacy muttered, shifting back to Hannah's side so that she was facing the tub again. "Steve Ericson and Sean Parker are at it again."

Hannah recognized the two men in profile, but she wouldn't have known their names. They were both from somewhere around Blackberry Valley, though she didn't think they lived in the town proper. Their surnames, however, were familiar when Lacy said them. They'd been mentioned in *Blackberry Secrets*. "Don't get along?" Then why had they stationed their kids beside each other?

"Oh no, they're best friends, when they're not swinging their fists at each other." Lacy shrugged.

"That's about what I'd expect from an Ericson," Sean barked. "None of you ever mind encroaching on what belongs to someone else."

"And what's that supposed to mean?"

"What, no one in your family has read that book yet? It confirms what my family's been claiming for generations—Rick Ericson moved the boundary stones and stole that whole stretch of land from my family."

Hannah hoped that Lacy was exaggerating with the "swinging fists" comment, but even if she was, the men were clearly more concerned with their argument than with the kids at their knees. One of the little boys dangled over the side of the pool as he strained for an apple, and his father was paying no attention whatsoever.

Hannah rushed forward, and Hailey clearly had the same instinct, because she was right beside Hannah, calling, "Don't lean so far over, honey!"

Hannah wasn't entirely sure what happened next. She knew she'd been reaching for the little boy, but the sudden appearance of two frantic women must have gotten the men's attention. They both jerked around as Hannah leaned over to catch the boy. The boy's father collided with her bent-over torso, and her awkward position meant she couldn't catch her balance. She lurched to the side, knocking into someone else. Then came another bump to her back, when her arms were busy trying not to send Hailey to the ground.

The next thing she knew, water closed in over her head, the side of the tub dug into her stomach, and someone had grabbed hold of her legs to stop her from going all the way into the apple tub. Other hands helped to haul her back out, and she spluttered, wiping water from her face and coughing as soon as she was in air again.

"Aw, man. I am so sorry," one of the men was saying.

"You okay, ma'am?" the other asked, helping Hailey to her feet. She'd apparently ended up partially submerged as well, given the water streaming from her hair and one entire arm up to her shoulder.

In response, Hailey burst into laughter. "Wow. That was refreshing."

Lacy appeared in Hannah's vision, a combination of horror and amusement on her face. "Are you all right?"

Hannah peeled her dripping hair off her face and smiled at the attendant who rushed their way with towels in hand. "I didn't melt in the water. I must not be made of sugar." Though she could still feel where the tub had dug into her stomach. She rubbed a hand over the spot.

Which of course made Lacy frown. "Want to go home?"

"Are you kidding? Now I need to walk around to dry off in the sun."

The attendant handed towels to both Hannah and Hailey, chiding the men for not paying enough attention as she did so.

Hannah stepped clear of the tub and the crowd of people who had gathered, happy to be able to bury her face in the towel for a moment. No doubt her cheeks were as red as Hailey's shirt.

She was still trying to soak up the water from her hair when her phone rang in her purse, making her pause in gratitude that her bag had been pinned between her body and the side of the tub, and hadn't gone into the water. When she pulled out her phone, John Comstock's name was on the screen. She answered and put the phone to her ear. "Hi, John. Thanks for getting back to me."

Lacy leaned in, pressing her ear to the other side of the phone.

"So, I was digging into this Annabeth Billings," John said without any preamble. "Found her marriage records from 1932, and I've got her children's names too."

Grinning, Hannah said, "That was fast."

"Haven't traced those kids' families yet to know who among us are their descendants. Do you want me to?"

When she'd reached out to John, she'd made it clear she wasn't asking as a favor, that she would pay him for his time. Which of course meant that the more time he put into it, the more she'd have to pay. She appreciated his asking. "Yes, please. But first, who did Annabeth marry?"

"Was it a Smith?" Lacy asked from her side of the phone.

John must not have had any trouble hearing her. "No, not a Smith. A Buchanan."

"As in, the Buchanan house? The place the whole book revolved around?" The Buchanans would have been one of the wealthiest families in Blackberry Valley at the time. Hannah pulled away enough to meet Lacy's eye.

Annabeth Billings had gone from being the poor friend, barefoot and threadbare, to marrying into one of the town's most well-to-do families?

Oh, there had to be a story there.

Chapter Seventeen

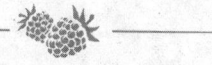

Blackberry Valley
May 1, 1936

Annabeth paused at the edge of town to fish her little notepad from her pocket, along with the stub of a pencil she'd shoved in there that morning. She'd woken up with story ideas swirling through her mind, making her wish she could stay home all day and tap out the next scenes in her book instead of going to the Buchanans' house.

Though now she was glad she'd gone. Mrs. Buchanan had decided that she wanted one of the spare rooms aired out and freshened up in case she brought her four-year-old granddaughter home with her when she returned from Louisville. Annabeth had never been in that room before, but as she was dusting and polishing, she'd found a half-door hidden behind the massive bed. Given its placement in the house, it was most likely an attic access.

But the fact that it had been hidden had given Annabeth all sorts of ideas. This would be her schoolmarm's bedroom. It would be arranged like this, but of course the teacher discovered the hidden door. And it had shown her far more than a few dusty relics in the attic. Max would have to discover them too. Whatever they ended up being.

She jotted down a few ideas for what the attic's secrets could be, staring up at the puffy white clouds drifting in the blue sky as she tried to remember some of the fleeting thoughts that had been buzzing through her mind as she finished up her work. Mrs. Buchanan had made sure she was gone well before her husband and son returned for lunch, so she had a few minutes to spare before Sue Ellen would expect her at the Adamses' place.

But instead of clues filtering into her mind, she saw Edwin Buchanan's face, the way he'd smiled at her last Saturday, outside her house. She hadn't seen him since, other than across the street on Wednesday. He'd waved and smiled, as had she, but he'd been with his mother, who had hustled him into another shop.

Mrs. Buchanan would be on the train to Louisville in another hour though. She wouldn't be back for weeks. She'd told Annabeth not to come to the house while she was gone, which had caused a moment of fluttering panic in her chest. Not doing that job for a month would mean a missing chunk of income.

On the other hand, some part of her she was afraid to examine whispered that maybe, with Mrs. Buchanan out of town, Edwin might find time to speak to her again. He could approach her after church. Or intercept her as she walked home one afternoon. Invite her for a soda or an ice cream.

They were silly dreams, better suited to a girl of sixteen than a woman of twenty-three who had to be practical. She knew that. Even if Edwin seemed to admire her for some reason, nothing could come of it. They were from two different worlds. And even if his father was a self-made man, his mother seemed like the sort to forbid a match between her son and a less-than-desirable woman. The sort who wanted to improve her social standing.

But that hadn't kept his handsome face from filling her mind at odd moments. Hadn't stopped her heart from warming whenever she thought of him sitting on one of those crude chairs Daddy had made, confessing his family's secrets and asking her to keep them.

She'd hurried to Sammy's first thing the next morning to tell her. Her best friend had not only been relieved to know that Edwin wasn't a thief, or worse, but she'd also been very quick to notice how Annabeth had softened toward him, and start the teasing.

It felt nice to be teased about someone. It felt *normal*, like what every other young woman got to experience. As she'd laughed with Sammy, she'd forgotten for a moment that she was wearing an old, barely serviceable cotton dress that was about two patches shy of the rag bin. She'd forgotten that her shoes had holes in the soles. She'd forgotten that half the town looked down their noses at her and the other half ignored her.

She'd been a girl with a crush on a boy, with a delicious feeling that maybe the boy had a crush on her too.

Annabeth shook it off and tucked her notepad back into her apron pocket. At this rate, she'd turn into a romance writer instead of a mystery writer. Though she'd likely only get a few chapters in before the whole thing would fizzle out and reality would sour all her imaginings. Edwin would turn his attention to someone better suited to him, Annabeth would hide her disappointment and shove those chapters into a drawer, and she'd go back to Max and murders and mysteries.

It wouldn't feel so hollow after a while. Right?

For now, she needed to stop woolgathering and get to the Adamses'.

She'd only gone a few more paces on the sidewalk before a loud voice from behind stopped her dead in her tracks.

"Stop right there! Don't go another step or I'll call the police on you, Annie Billings!"

Mrs. Buchanan? Dread cinching tight in her belly, Annabeth turned slowly around. She had no idea why her employer would threaten her with the police, but it couldn't be good.

Suddenly she was eight again, her hand engulfed in her father's as they walked down this very street on some errand or another. It was a male voice shouting at them, claiming Daddy had stolen something in the shop they'd just come out of. People had crowded around. The police had come.

Never mind that his pockets had been empty. They'd searched *hers* too, and she keenly remembered the humiliation of it. Not just at the search, but also at the rough hands holding her still.

Her pockets had holes in them. And the shopkeeper had sneered and said the stolen goods had probably fallen out, but that their empty state didn't prove they hadn't taken the items. Her eyes wanted to burn now at the memory as they had then. At the lesson she'd learned that day.

Poverty was all the proof some people needed of criminal intent.

Mrs. Buchanan's eyes were agleam with manic light as she came to a puffing halt a few feet away. She was a lovely woman, generally speaking. The same blue eyes her son boasted, chestnut hair threaded with elegant silver. But just now, she looked half-crazed, hair tumbling free of its pins and no hat on her head—something Annabeth had never seen her without when away from the house.

Her throat went tight. "What's the matter, Mrs. Buchanan?"

"What's the matter?" The woman straightened her shoulders, fury etching lines in her face. "I'll tell you what's the matter. You've robbed us! Taken it all!"

The dread hollowed her stomach into a pit. An inkling of what was going on wormed its way into her mind. "I haven't taken anything." She kept her voice low, calm, holding out her arms, inviting her employer to see that she had nothing on her to allow for the removal of the stacks of cash in her husband's safe. No bag, no basket, no bucket, no box. Nothing but an apron whose pockets held only the money that had been left for her on the kitchen table.

But Mrs. Buchanan obviously couldn't hear reason. She took another step forward, lifting a shaking finger to poke at Annabeth. "What have you done with it? Where have you hidden it? I *know* you took it. You're the only one who's been in the house. And you peek in every corner, don't you? Move every piece of furniture. You probably found where he'd written down the combination to the safe."

Heads poked out of windows. Bodies emerged from shops. Annabeth didn't dare figure out who was witnessing this. Who would now look at her and think *thief*, just because the accusation had been made.

But she wasn't. She'd never taken a thing in her life that didn't belong to her. Mrs. Buchanan was the one who had lost all of her family's money, who might steal from her own daughter, who—

Who was broken. In the grips of an addiction she couldn't control. It gleamed there in her eyes, that unfettered monster gnashing her in its teeth. But there was a woman behind the monster, frantic and screaming to be set free.

Peace, cool and calm, washed over Annabeth as she saw in Mrs. Buchanan's eyes something she recognized all too well—desperation. The verses she'd read that morning in Romans sprang into her mind.

She needed to bless this woman who was trying to persecute her. She needed to mourn with her. She needed to do more than watch and observe and write it all down—she needed to take an actual part in the grieving, the rejoicing. Instead of railing that the people of Blackberry Valley judged her too quickly, refused to associate with her because she was of low standing, Annabeth had to be vulnerable enough to show them who she really was.

And she needed to be someone worth knowing. Someone like Sammy, filled with compassion. Someone like Pru, always ready with a smile.

Maybe that was where it started, somehow. With a woman trying to ruin her because it was easier than admitting her own problems. *Lord, give me Your wisdom. Give me Your love.* Her own had never been enough.

But she had more than her own to draw on. She eased a step closer to Mrs. Buchanan and kept her voice low and soft. "Ma'am, I have never so much as touched your husband's safe. I respect your family and what you've built. I would never want to harm you by stealing. You've blessed me so much by giving me good, honest work and paying me well for it. I wouldn't abuse that."

Mrs. Buchanan shook her head wildly. "It was you. I ought not to have taken you on just because Bess Adams recommended you. You've probably been stealing from them all your life. I know your type—conniving, scheming. You think I don't see how your mind is whirring while you're scrubbing floors? How you reach for your notebook all the time? Writing down what you plan to take next, I don't doubt."

Annabeth went still. She was keenly aware that the notebook in her pocket did indeed have some scheming in it that might look suspicious to the police if they demanded to see it. Including notes on what may have been stolen from the Buchanan house and hidden in their attic—and how it could lead to a dead body.

Would the authorities believe her if she told them it was nothing more than ideas for a novel? She could even show them the typed pages. But that was the last thing she wanted to do. Those pages still held her neighbors' real names, their real stories. She meant to change it all enough to be pure fiction in the next draft, but that wouldn't help her now.

Panic broke through the calm, clawing at her throat. She had never meant for anyone to see her notes, her words, her stories in their current form. Not when those words could hurt them, humiliate them in some cases. Cause rifts between families in others. That had never been her intention at all.

She couldn't offer up the book as proof, if they demanded it. Couldn't explain away the notes in her pocket if it meant harming others.

She would have to trust that justice would prevail. The truth was that she hadn't taken the money and didn't know where it was. That truth would have to protect her.

To Mrs. Buchanan she said, "I'm just a daydreamer, ma'am. Jotting down my musings as I have them, worthless as they are to anyone else. But if you'd feel better calling the police, you go ahead. I'll stay right here."

Footsteps sounded behind her, and at Mrs. Buchanan's look of victory, she expected a uniformed officer to grip her arm at any moment and drag her down to the station. Instead, Edwin stepped to Annabeth's side and touched a gentle hand to her elbow. "Mother? What's going on here?"

That finger waved at her again. "I'll tell you what's going on. This beggar robbed us blind. She took every last dollar from your father's safe."

Edwin sighed. She could all but hear him thinking, *We were so close. Just an hour more, and she'd have been on the train.* "And how do you know that?" He asked it softly, gently. Clearly meaning to jar her back into rationality by inviting her to remember what no one else on the street would know—that she shouldn't have been able to open that safe and see its empty state, because her husband couldn't trust her with the combination.

Mrs. Buchanan's face flushed scarlet. She sputtered but said nothing.

Edwin eased a step closer. "I'm the one who moved the money from the safe, Mother. It's nothing to be alarmed about. Miss Billings didn't take anything."

His mother shook her head. "No. No, she got her claws into you. I've seen how you look at her. She put you up to this. She—"

"That's enough." Again, his tone was heartbreakingly gentle as he spoke, just as his touch was obviously feather-soft as he clasped his mother's elbow. "We'd better get home if you hope to make the train on time. All right?"

Annabeth felt rather than saw the crowd shift, some stepping out of the way, but some drawing nearer. For a moment, she wondered what they'd do. Pretend they hadn't seen anything? Scowl at her, thinking that Edwin was indeed lying to protect her?

Or perhaps, if they'd heard the madness in Mrs. Buchanan's tone as clearly as she had, they'd judge her unstable and avoid her gaze lest they be drawn into her delusions.

Mrs. Johnston stepped up to Mrs. Buchanan's other side and wrapped a sturdy arm around her waist. Her face was every bit as soft and caring as Edwin's. "Let me walk home with you, Vickie. Did I ever tell you about the time I misplaced the pearl earrings my parents had given me for my wedding? I thought for sure the handyman had taken them when he repainted our bedroom. Turned out, I'd put them in the icebox in an exhausted haze when I went to pour some milk for the baby. The icebox of all places!" She laughed at herself and urged Mrs. Buchanan around—then sent a wink toward Edwin behind his mother's back.

The thick, old wall around Annabeth's heart cracked. Crumbled.

And collapsed altogether when an arm slid around her own waist. Hannah Jane Prentiss murmured at her side. "Sometimes people say silly things when their nerves are stretched to the limit, don't they? I bet she gets anxious when she travels, and I don't blame her. She probably went to get a bit of spending money for her trip, and when she didn't find it where she thought it should be, she was in too much of a frazzle to think straight. I can't imagine any other reason she'd blame you. Everyone in this town knows you'd never take so much as a crumb that didn't belong to you, Annie. Bess Adams recommended you because you're a good woman, and she was right."

Warmth blossomed like spring flowers where that wall had been. "Thank you for saying so." Her smile wobbled a bit around the edges, but she offered it all the same. "But you can bet I ate every last crumb of those cookies you sent home with me the other day. Never had better. Would you share your recipe, or is it a secret?"

Hannah Jane's eyes lit at the compliment. "Did you like them? My mother-in-law hinted that they were dry. Insisted on dunking hers in her coffee."

There it was—the insecurity that must have sent *her* into a frazzle before her husband's birthday party. "I thought they were perfect. I'm sure your mother-in-law likes the blend of sweet and bitter she got from dipping them in her coffee."

"That's so kind of you to say." Hannah Jane gave her waist a squeeze. "I would be delighted to share my recipe."

Edwin shifted into her view. She'd thought he'd be escorting his mother home, but Mrs. Johnston was walking her down the street toward the proud house at the end of it. He paused when he spotted her, twisting his hat in his hands.

Hannah Jane cleared her throat and stepped away. "You have a good weekend, Annie. I'll see you later."

"You too, Mrs. Prentiss."

"Enough of that. You call me Hannah Jane, like everyone else. We're all neighbors here." She moved off, as most of the other onlookers had too. Annabeth would bet that Hannah Jane had no idea how much those few words meant to her.

Edwin offered her his arm. "May I walk you to wherever you're going, Miss Billings?"

"It's Annabeth." Much as she wanted to tuck her hand into the crook of his elbow, she held back. Mrs. Buchanan was displeased enough with her. "Shouldn't you see your mother home?"

He didn't so much as glance over his shoulder. "My father will catch up with them."

She hadn't even noticed the elder Mr. Buchanan, but now that Edwin mentioned it, she spotted the gentleman striding toward the two women. And when she returned her gaze to Edwin's face, she read determination there. He wouldn't disrespect her, but he did seem to need to say something to her.

So she nodded, turned back in the direction she'd been going before his mother stopped her, and rested her hand on his forearm. "I was just on my way to the Adamses' house."

He nodded, not speaking as they passed the remaining buildings in town. But once they were on the road to the large house on the hill, he drew in a long breath. "I can't thank you enough for responding to her with grace and calm. You could have defended yourself with the truth."

"I did. I told her I didn't take the money."

He shot her a smile. "You know what I mean. There are those who wouldn't have hesitated to proclaim for all to hear that *she* was the reason the money wasn't there. Pointed out that she would take it to gamble."

Annabeth had to look away from his warm blue eyes before they melted her. "I promised I wouldn't say anything."

"When I asked that favor, I didn't realize my mother would accuse you of a crime in the street like that. I would never ask you to keep our secret at a cost to yourself." His voice, so soft and deep, lured her gaze right back to him.

"I appreciate that, but it wasn't my secret to tell."

She peered behind them at the town she'd been so sure was judging her. Waiting to condemn her for even a whisper of a mistake.

But that wasn't what had happened mere moments before. She'd seen neighbors who recognized a wrong and who wanted to help make it right. Who humbled themselves to put others at ease. Who tried to shore up the weak places.

"I think maybe you aren't giving everyone enough credit," she said to Edwin. "I understand not wanting the world to know about your mother's struggles. But if they knew, they could support you. They could pray for her. Maybe that would be more helpful than trying to keep it secret."

He was silent long enough that she wondered if it had been the wrong thing to say and she should have kept the thought to herself. But then he covered her fingers with his free hand and gave them a squeeze. "I'll admit that's a terrifying thought. We had friends in Louisville who found out and wouldn't speak to my mother anymore. But we *are* called to confess to one another, to share one another's joys and sorrows. Perhaps if we could confide in a few people we could trust to pray for her, that might help lighten our load."

"I can't predict whether it would go well or badly. But know that *I* will be praying. I should have been already. I'm sorry I didn't think to." She'd been too caught up in herself, in her story, in the excitement of Edwin's attention. But after seeing that desperation in his mother's eyes, she wouldn't forget Mrs. Buchanan in her prayers now.

"I appreciate that more than you can know. And please know that we aren't trying to cover up anything so that she can get away with it. My father has made certain all her debts are paid, and she has admitted her wrongdoing and repented. Yet there's still something that compels her. I don't understand it, but I know she fights against it every day. She can do well for years, and then it's like something overpowers her. You saw today how that can be. It makes her frantic, blinds her temporarily to right and wrong."

Annabeth didn't pretend to understand it either, not completely. But she'd seen the compulsion for herself. And though this struggle of his mother's was interior, perhaps it wasn't so different from when one's external circumstances caused a constant fight. When something beyond one's control had a person in its teeth, it could feel like there was no way out. And that she understood. "I think it's to your credit that you and your father try to protect her in this. And I will be praying that its grip on her loosens for good."

"Thank you." They walked in silence for a minute. When the gates to the Adams property loomed directly ahead, he looked at her again, and his eyes were lighter, his smile brighter. "May I ask you a nosy question?"

Her brows lifted. "You can ask. Though if it's *too* nosy, I may not answer."

His grin didn't falter. "What *do* you write all the time in that notepad of yours?"

The way he said it—like he'd seen her pull it out and jot things down on multiple occasions—made her cheeks heat. When had he noticed such a little thing? Had he really been watching her enough to see her do it more than once? "It's nothing."

"Annabeth."

Hearing her name on his lips again made a little thrill shoot through her. Which was probably why she told him the truth. "Just story ideas."

He rewarded her honesty with a beaming smile. "You're a writer?"

"Fiction. Nothing serious. Writing helps me work through things. Dreaming up stories keeps my mind occupied while my hands are busy."

"Maybe someday you'll let me read something you've written."

Assuming she wrote something worth sharing. "Maybe someday."

Chapter Eighteen

"Are there even any Buchanans left in the area?" Hailey pinched a bite of cotton candy from the cone they were sharing and offered the rest to Hannah and Lacy.

Hannah tore free some of the treat too, still amused that the designer-wearing minor celebrity was walking around the fairgrounds with them, licking spun sugar off her fingers while the three of them compared notes. "All I know is that the Hanes family now owns the old Buchanan house. Any ideas, Lacy?"

Her friend paused, deep in thought, but ended up shrugging. "Not that I know of. I mean, I don't know *everyone* in town, but I think I'd remember hearing the name Buchanan."

"Maybe that part of the book is true too. Maybe someone really did steal all their money, and they ended up losing the house and left town or something. What's going on over there?" Hailey pointed toward a large crowd of people gathered around something Hannah couldn't make out.

"I don't think that theory about the Buchanans fits," Hannah said. "According to Alice Tyler, there are photos of Pru Tyler with Annabeth and their other friend going back decades."

"Doesn't mean they all lived here forever though," Lacy pointed out. "We have plenty of pictures of us from when you were living in

California, Hannah. From when you came to visit, or when I went to see you out there."

Hannah could grant that point. "True enough."

"It would be so much fun if there was money buried somewhere outside of town," Hailey said around another mouthful of dissolving sugar. "There was that book a few years ago where the author really did go bury gems all over the country, commissioned an artist to paint pictures with clues hidden in them, wrote up more clues, and published it? This could be like that. The author knew of the real treasure and planted the clues. Y'all can go treasure hunting, and I'll be there with a film crew to record it. *That* would be a fun story to cover."

Hannah shook her head. "Would you seriously rather cover the story than be part of the treasure hunt?"

"Absolutely." Hailey grinned. "Especially if everyone *fails* to find it, so it's an ongoing story I can revisit from time to time."

The crowd of people all held paper bowls, and as they drew closer, Hannah saw that they'd gathered around a giant apple pie. It was the size of a merry-go-round. According to the sign she was now close enough to read, fifty bushels of apples had gone into the pie, along with a hundred and fifty pounds of sugar, fifteen pounds of butter, a pound and a half of cinnamon, and more.

Lacy let out a whistle. "How did they bake that?"

"The pan does the cooking," Hailey said as she waved the cotton candy at a woman who could have been her older sister, wearing an apron and a badge. "Took twelve hours though. Mom was afraid it would never actually get done."

The woman dodged through the crowd to join them. "There you are," she said with a smile. "Have you seen your father since he finished? I can't find him anywhere."

"He was standing in line for barbecue, last I saw him." Hailey gestured to them. "Mom, this is Hannah and Lacy, from Blackberry Valley. Hannah owns that restaurant we said we were going to try on Tuesday, and Lacy runs a farm that supplies fresh eggs to local businesses and individuals. Ladies, this is my mom, Abigail Cassidy."

They exchanged greetings, then Abigail said, "You girls want some pie? Let me grab a few bowls." She trotted away without waiting for an answer.

Hailey chuckled. "Don't bother saying no. She's so proud of that pie that you could tell her you hate apples and she'd still make you try it."

"This would be a really sad place to be if you hated apples." Hannah spotted a cluster of people from town and waved. "Luckily, I am pro apple pie."

Tracy Galloway waved back, which cued the rest of the group to turn to see who'd caught her attention. Wyatt was there with his wife, Sandy, and Evangeline Cook stood with her husband, Ted. The group moved toward them, reaching them as Abigail returned with three bowls of pie.

"Nice turnout this year, isn't it?" Wyatt asked Abigail. Hannah couldn't tell if they knew each other or if he'd simply seen her badge and knew she was on staff.

Hannah spooned a bite of pie into her mouth and nearly cheered in delight at the burst of cinnamon and sugar, which enhanced the rich apple flavor.

"Best yet." Hailey's mom surveyed the crowd with clear pride. "I keep telling my daughter that she should have brought her film crew and covered it for the morning show."

"Bet that fight would have gotten you all the ratings." Lacy grinned at Hannah and Hailey.

Abigail frowned. "You two were fighting?"

Hannah and Hailey both burst into laughter. Lacy clarified. "No, I'm exaggerating. There was an argument between a couple dads, and they weren't paying attention to one of their kids trying to take a swim. When Hannah and Hailey tried to keep the little boy on dry land, they ended up unintentionally bobbing for apples."

The intervening hour had been hot enough to dry their hair and shirts, but Hannah hadn't been brave enough to find a mirror and see what state her hair might be in. Hailey was somehow still immaculate as she tossed the now-empty cotton candy cone into the trash and dug into her pie.

"Oh, there's your father," Abigail said to her daughter. "Brad! Over here, honey."

"I knew I recognized you," Tracy said to Hailey. "Hailey Cassidy, right? I love your show. I'd forgotten you were from around here though. Home for the festival?"

Hailey smiled as she swallowed a bite of pie. "Yep. Had to come see all Mom's efforts pay off. Hey, Dad."

"Hey, sweet pea." Brad Cassidy carried a paper tray that held a half-eaten barbecue sandwich. He looked to be about sixty, with a trim gray beard but hair still more pepper than salt. He wore a T-shirt with YONDER VALLEY BLUEGRASS BAND on it. "You see that tent with signed copies of *Blackberry Secrets*? Think the author's around?"

"We already checked," Hannah said. "The booth belongs to a bookseller the author shipped the books to. The author isn't there."

Brad took a sip of the lemonade he held. "Too bad. I'd have liked to tell B.B. Smith where he messed up."

Hannah exchanged a glance with Lacy.

Hailey groaned. "Dad, you do *not* greet an author with a list of their mistakes and oversights. I mean, unless you want to be blacklisted by all authors everywhere."

Sandy Granger beat Hannah to the question she was dying to ask. "Where did B.B. mess up?"

"The church." Brad passed his lemonade to his wife to hold so he had a free hand to lift his sandwich.

The rest of them all stared at him for a moment, waiting for him to go on, but he took a bite instead.

Wyatt finally gave a prod. "The church has been in Blackberry Valley since its founding."

Brad swallowed and put his sandwich down again. "Sure. But not that building. The original burnt to the ground in 1939. New one wasn't finished until '41. But it's the current building described in the book. The original didn't have a bell, only a steeple. The book has the church bells ringing out."

Was this guy a historian as well as a banjo player? Hannah shook her head. "You just happen to know this?" They didn't live in Blackberry Valley.

Brad smiled. "My grandfather was the pastor of the church at the time. He and Grammy Sam were nearly killed in the fire, which spread to the parsonage. They got out, but things were touch and go with Grammy for a while. She was pregnant with my dad and nearly lost him. So of course that story was trotted out regularly over the years."

Hannah's mind had caught on *Grammy Sam*. "Sam as in Samantha? Samantha Adams, perhaps?" Even as she asked, she studied Hailey—those striking features, the bright blond hair.

She'd been searching for a resemblance to the wrong person from that photograph. Hailey might not look anything like Annabeth Billings, but she looked quite a bit like Samantha Adams. How had she missed that before?

Brad blinked at her. "That's right. Do you know of her?"

"I saw her in a photo with Pru Tyler and Annabeth Billings. Alice Tyler was setting up a display about her husband's family in the library."

He nodded. "The Tylers are good people. Of course, all their neighbors were. They really rallied around my grandparents after the fire. They lost everything, but they always said they were never allowed to feel it for a moment."

Hailey turned to them. "You know that big old house just outside of Blackberry Valley? The one being renovated now? That's where Grammy Sam grew up."

"I had no idea you actually had ties *in* Blackberry Valley," Tracy said as Hannah's phone rang.

After handing her empty bowl to Lacy, Hannah stepped away from the group and pulled her phone out of her purse. John's name and number were on the screen again. Smiling, she answered with, "You really don't have to do all this research for me on a Sunday afternoon."

"It's fun," he assured her. "Besides, I'm procrastinating grading some research papers."

"Research papers so soon in the year? You are not the fun teacher, are you?"

John laughed. "In my defense, they only had to be two pages. But let's not tell the kids that I'm putting off grading them as surely as they put off writing them."

"Your secret is safe with me."

"Much obliged. Anyway, this project is pretty interesting. So, Annabeth and Edwin had three kids, all girls, which means no one still around with the Buchanan surname. One of the daughters, Josephine, married and moved to Washington, so I didn't imagine you were too interested in that branch of the family."

"Probably not." When laughter from the group filled her ears, she wandered another step away to better hear. "What about the other two daughters?"

"The oldest is Judith, who married Ron Malone. Their kids, of course, are Brian and Tracy."

He said it like she should know who they are. And maybe she did. "Tracy, as in Tracy Galloway?"

"Yep. And the youngest of their girls was Lucille, who married Jonathan Granger."

"Granger." Her eyes went wide. "Wyatt? Wyatt and Tracy are cousins?"

"Well, yeah. You didn't know that?"

"I've been gone a long time, John. I almost forgot you and Jim were brothers."

"Easy to do. We look nothing alike," he joked. "Wyatt's sisters have moved away, as has Brian Malone. Leaving Tracy and Wyatt in town from Annabeth's line. Is there anything else I can do for you?"

"I think so." Her mind was still spinning. Wyatt and Tracy had both been full of ideas about how to capitalize on the fame the book was bringing Blackberry Valley. Both were well educated, articulate, and creative. She wouldn't be surprised to learn that either was a closet novelist. For all she knew, they both might be. They could have worked on the book together.

"Am I allowed to be nosy and ask why you're so interested in Annabeth? I thought at first maybe she was one of your ancestors."

Hannah debated for a moment. If Wyatt or Tracy had written the book, they'd also gone to great lengths to preserve their privacy. And John had been pretty put out with the author when people had thought it was him. She didn't know if his thoughts had softened in that regard, but she didn't want to cause any rifts. Especially when she hadn't verified which of them it was. If either.

For now, it seemed wisest to hedge. "My great-grandmother mentioned an Annie in her journals, and then I saw a photo with Annabeth in it, along with a Pru Tyler. I was curious. What do I owe you?"

"Fifty bucks sound fair?" John asked.

"No way. You spent all afternoon on it," Hannah protested.

"I'm giving you a friends-and-family discount, since the project was so fascinating. Any time you're curious, you know how to find me."

"Thanks, John." She disconnected, slid her phone back into her bag, and pivoted. She'd pull Tracy and Wyatt aside and get to the bottom of this, once and for all.

But her determination didn't last long. The group had broken up. Only Lacy and the Cassidys were still there. Scan the crowds as she might, Hannah couldn't see the Blackberry Valley contingent anywhere. She moved back to Lacy's side. "Where did the others go?"

"Heading home," Lacy said around a yawn. "They said to tell you goodbye. And I think they have the right idea. I'm wiped. You?"

She actually felt rather excited with the new information buzzing through her mind, but that didn't mean she wasn't ready to head back to town. She sent Liam a quick text, letting him know that they were going home rather than re-joining him and his grandfather, and asking him to pass on her apologies. "I'm good to go whenever you're ready."

"You're leaving already? Here." Hailey shoved her now-empty pie bowl into her mother's hands and reached into her pocket. She pulled out a slender metal business card holder and removed a card. "If you figure out where the treasure's buried, give me a call so I can cover it. And we'll see you Tuesday night at the Hot Spot."

"Sounds good." Hannah slid the card into her purse as she and Lacy said their farewells to Hailey and her parents.

As they walked back to Lacy's truck, Hannah brought her friend up-to-date on the information John had passed along.

Lacy whistled low. "So either Wyatt or Tracy must be B.B. Smith."

"Assuming we're right about the Annabeth Billings connection."

"Well, rats. Had I known, I wouldn't have let them walk away. Whose door do you want to knock on first when we get back to town?"

Hannah laughed and moved around to her side of the truck. "According to your theory, B.B.'s a guy, so Wyatt's?"

Lacy unlocked the doors, and they both climbed in. "Are we really going to do that? I don't know where either of them lives, exactly. General neighborhoods, but not actual addresses."

Hannah considered. While chasing leads was fun and she really wanted answers, she didn't have their addresses either. And it seemed a little weird to show up and make accusations. "Let's skip the door-knocking idea. I'm sure we'll see them around town soon enough."

Lacy started the truck and held up a fist for bumping. "Good sleuthing today, Prentiss. We make awesome super spies."

With a laugh, Hannah touched her knuckles to her friend's. "That we do, Minyard. That we do."

Chapter Nineteen

Though she hadn't felt tired when they left the fairgrounds, the motion of the truck lulled Hannah into drowsiness in minutes. The combination of sun, walking, and way too much food all conspired against her. By the time they reached the Blackberry Valley town limits, conversation had petered out and she was staring out the window, watching the world roll by.

Her gaze tracked to the church steeple, that new nugget of information swirling through her mind as the lowering sun glinted off the bell. She traced the line of the tower down to the roof, along the familiar structure of the building, to the parking lot, empty but for one lone SUV.

"Wait! Turn in, turn in!" Hannah clung to the handle above the window while Lacy, ever a good friend, wheeled into the church parking lot without even asking why.

At least before she did it. Once off the road, she asked, "What? Why?" Then she spotted the SUV and let out a laugh. "He had to come check it out. Gotcha, Wyatt." She swung her truck into a parking spot, and they both unlatched their seat belts and scrambled from the vehicle.

The front of the church was empty, but when they followed the sidewalk around the corner, they found Wyatt and Sandy standing between two bushes.

Hannah grinned. "Is that where the date marker is? Fact-checking Brad Cassidy—or maybe wishing someone had fact-checked you, B.B.?"

Wyatt spun around at her voice, a quick succession of emotions chasing over his face. A rueful smile was the last to settle. "Figured it out, did you?"

She laughed and stopped on the sidewalk behind them, hoping her posture conveyed that, to them, it was all in good fun. "I wasn't sure if it was you or Tracy."

He tilted his head. "How did you know it was either of us?"

"Annabeth Billings." Lacy motioned toward Hannah. "Hannah Jane Prentiss mentioned her in a journal entry. With the cookie jar story."

"In which it was Annabeth where Max stood in the novel. I figured she was the only other one who really knew that story, so B.B. Smith must have gotten it from her somehow. A descendant made the most sense."

Sandy patted his arm. "Told you someone would figure it out eventually, sweetheart."

"Yes, you did." Wyatt let out a long sigh. "Thought I'd have longer than a month of anonymity, though."

"We won't tell anyone if you don't want us to." Hannah shifted out of the way so Wyatt and Sandy could emerge from the bushes. "I wasn't trying to figure it out to do a big exposé or anything. I mostly wanted to thank you for bringing Hannah Jane to life. And let you know that if others *do* figure it out, I've got your back."

Wyatt's shoulders relaxed a bit. "I appreciate that, Hannah. I honestly didn't expect the kind of outrage I've seen from some people. I thought the way Gran portrayed everyone was so well done."

Lacy stepped forward. "Wait. The way *she* portrayed them?"

His smile went wistful. "The novel was hers. Mostly. She wrote it before she and my grandfather got married, though she never finished it. Left it with a chapter to go. She let me read it when I was a boy, and when I asked her why she never finished or published it, she said her reasons for writing it changed, and she lost interest in telling the story. She said she always knew if she did anything with it, she'd have to fictionalize all the names and make things less *real*. And it was more fun to move on to new stories. So she left that one in a drawer."

"Wow." Hannah shook her head. "So did she publish other stuff? Books, stories?"

"She wrote quite a few short stories that were published in magazines over the years. A couple other novels that she always said weren't ready." His wry smile said he didn't agree with that assessment. "I think what it came down to was that she wrote them for herself, not for anyone else. I couldn't argue with that."

"Wyatt's been writing for years too," Sandy said with obvious pride. "Don't let him convince you that book was all his grandmother. He used her plot, characters, and descriptions, but completely rewrote it according to modern sensibilities. And, of course, came up with the ending."

"Joint effort," he said. "Made me feel like I was sitting with Gran every time I worked on it. Like she was there with me."

Hannah rested her hand over her heart. "I love that. Especially because when I read the words about my great-grandmother, that's how I felt. As if she was here with me. A younger version of her that I never had the chance to know, but can now thanks to your book."

"Okay, I have to know," Lacy said. "Where did you get your pseudonym? Does it mean something?"

Wyatt grinned. "B.B. is for Billings and Buchanan, Gran's two last names. And I chose Smith because she always said I was a wordsmith like her. I thought it was fitting."

"Plus," Sandy added, "it's so common a surname that it wouldn't give anyone any clues. I kept trying to tell him to use his own name."

"That didn't feel right, not when so much of the book wasn't mine." Wyatt shrugged. "I might have tried harder to hide it if I'd realized I'd need the protection from my own neighbors. I honestly thought everyone would get a kick out of seeing their ancestors in there. Otherwise I would have changed the names. Gran was right about that."

Sandy nudged his arm. "Tell them your plan, sweetheart."

"Plan?" Hannah straightened.

Wyatt held Sandy's gaze for a moment, a silent conversation passing between them. Then he grinned. "We could use the help, I suppose."

"For what?" Lacy demanded.

Wyatt raised an eyebrow. "For the treasure hunt."

This time, Hannah and Lacy were the ones to exchange a look that spoke for them. Hannah recognized the excitement in Lacy's eyes, which was probably mirrored in her own. "You mean the treasure from the book?" Hannah asked.

"It's *real*?" Lacy added.

"Well, funny story," Wyatt said, laughing. "It *was* real, after a fashion. My grandmother caught my grandfather burying his family's money in a field outside of town. At the request of his father, he was hiding it from his mother, who had a gambling problem. His mother was supposed to go to Louisville to support his sister while she had a baby, and it so happened that it was around the time of the Kentucky Derby. His father wanted to remove the temptation."

Hannah had no words to express how that made her feel. "Wow."

"I agree. I don't know of many men back in that day who would stay with a woman who put their livelihood in danger, but it sounds like Edwin's parents truly loved each other. His mother did eventually get a handle on her addiction, I'm happy to say."

Sandy gave a peaceful sigh. "I always loved that story. Annabeth thought he'd stolen something and that, when he realized she'd seen him, he was out to buy her silence."

"She avoided him for weeks." Wyatt motioned for Hannah and Lacy to follow as he started back toward the parking lot. "But he finally cornered her and told her the real story. Anyway, the money's obviously not still buried anywhere. But I did make sure the description in the book leads to a real place, if people are paying enough attention."

"Are you sure?" Lacy asked. "Because I know a lot of people are trying to figure it out, and I haven't heard that anyone thinks they have it yet."

"I told you that you made it too complicated." Sandy swatted his arm.

"Yes, dear," Wyatt said with mock exasperation. "Anyway, I have a solution. I'll pretend that *I* figured it out, make a case for it, and invite people along. It'll still work fine." He headed toward his car and popped the trunk. From a box in the back, he pulled out one of the maps of Blackberry Valley that he'd had made for the tourists. After closing the trunk again, he set the map on it and tapped his finger on a place at the edge of town. "This is where Gran caught Pap burying the money. The Buchanans owned this field at the time."

"But, unfortunately, the family doesn't own that land anymore," Sandy added.

"So instead of the historical burial site, I decided to make the cash in the book be buried out here." He tapped a second place, on the opposite edge of town. "At the far edge of our property, the other side of where the power lines divide it. I figured most people don't even realize we still own this tract of land. It's mostly undeveloped. But there are some notable landmarks, including an oak tree that has to be a couple hundred years old. I figured that's where we'll bury it."

"The original site was at an oak too," Sandy added.

Hannah lifted her brows. "But I assume you're not burying cash."

His grin was boyish. "No, I have a different treasure in mind. I won't ruin the surprise for you, but I could use some help spreading the word. I'm hoping this will pull the community together, since I unwittingly did some damage there."

"Just tell us what we can do to help," Lacy said.

Hannah pulled Hailey's business card from her purse. "And do you by chance want some media coverage for this?"

***

Both Hannah and Lacy were yawning by the time they reached the gravel drive leading to Bluegrass Hollow Farm. They pulled up to the farmhouse, which was mostly dark save for the living room. Neil was probably in there reading. Or writing. Or poring over yet another map.

Lacy parked in her usual spot. "Want to come in?"

"Thanks, but I'm beat. I want to get home." Hannah reached for her purchases from the festival, including the watercolor painting she loved. "Don't forget Neil's dumpling."

"Oh, right." Lacy grabbed the container, along with her own treasures.

They both climbed down and met at the front of the truck for a hug.

"Thanks for a great day, Lacy. I needed it."

"I know you did, and honestly so did I. It was fun." Lacy gave her a squeeze and then released her. "I can't believe we actually figured out who B.B. is."

"Me neither. But I'm curious about this treasure. What do you think he's up to?"

"I have no idea. We'll know soon enough." Lacy took a step toward the house. "I'll stop over tomorrow sometime, and we can figure out where to hang your new painting."

"I'll make us lunch."

"Perfect. See you then."

"Night." Hannah fished her keys from her purse, loaded her things into the back seat of her car, and climbed into the front. They'd ended up chatting in the church parking lot with the Grangers for an hour, going over Wyatt's plan to get the town involved in his treasure hunt and then listening to his story about finding a literary agent and publisher, and how surprised he'd been when the book took off so quickly. He didn't have actual sales data yet, but knowing that his grandmother's book had made it onto the bestseller charts was gratifying.

Tired as she was, Hannah hadn't been able to bring herself to cut the conversation short. It had felt special to be the first ones to get those stories from a neighbor whose hard work had been successful. But she was definitely feeling the weight of exhaustion now.

By the time she finally climbed the stairs to her apartment, she was having a serious internal debate about whether she most wanted a shower or to collapse on the couch for a while. It was still too early for bed, but her legs were tired enough that the couch won. She set the painting on the table and stretched out.

She nearly reached for the TV remote, but grabbed *Blackberry Secrets* instead. They'd eventually decided that instead of Wyatt being the one to "solve" the mystery of where the money was buried, Hannah and Lacy would do it. Wyatt had walked them through the clues verbally and promised to send them an email with the details all written out the next day, but Hannah flipped through the book to see if she could find the hints he'd mentioned.

She didn't mean to start reading, to get caught up again in the story. But one of the clues had come in another scene with Hannah Jane. Someone accused Max of being behind the crimes rather than trying to solve them, and Hannah Jane was his unexpected champion. She stepped forward and stood up for him, claiming that everybody knew he was trustworthy.

It had been an apology, even without the words "I'm sorry." Max knew it as surely as the reader did.

It made her wonder if a similar exchange had ever happened between her great-grandmother and Annabeth Billings. There'd been no other entries from 1936 in the journal Maeve scanned, no other mention of "Annie" in later years at all. But it rang true for the woman Hannah had heard so many stories about.

After getting through that scene again, Hannah didn't want to hunt for the rest of the clues anymore. She simply hugged the book to her chest with the image of Hannah Jane burning bright in her heart, a beacon that inspired Hannah to be more like her great-grandmother.

Chapter Twenty

Hannah stood on the porch of the old Buchanan house, Lacy and Neil on one side of her, Dad and Uncle Gordon on the other. She gazed over the milling crowd of residents who had turned out on this sunny Saturday morning for the treasure hunt, happy to see that nearly all the families mentioned in the book were represented. And she was pretty sure at least one or two tourists had joined the crowd too.

"Thanks again for letting us start here," Lacy said to their hosts.

Claire and Josh Hanes smiled. "No big deal at all," Josh said, elbowing his wife with a grin. "The big deal comes later."

Claire chuckled, though she looked a bit distracted. And no wonder. They were hosting the open house Josh had wanted from noon until six. Hannah fully intended to pop in after the hunt before she had to be back at the restaurant.

"If you need any help with last-minute details, we should have some time to spare between the end of the hunt and when your open house starts," Hannah told Claire quietly. "I can lend a hand."

Claire focused her gaze on Hannah, giving her a smile. "Thanks. I *think* we have everything ready, but if something comes up, I'll let you know."

From the sidewalk in front of the house, Alice Tyler asked, "What are we waiting for? Looks like everyone who wants to come is here."

Not quite everyone. Hannah had been a bit surprised when she'd arrived twenty minutes before and seen that Hailey and her crew weren't there yet—until she got a text from the journalist saying they'd had a flat tire an hour out of Louisville and were running behind. Still coming, but they'd be rolling in right around ten. Hannah would have to stall everyone until they got there.

She smiled at Alice. "I know of a couple more people who are coming from out of town. They had car trouble."

"But there they are." Lacy pointed down the street at a big white van with the Louisville news station's call sign and the name of Hailey's morning show on the side panels.

Hannah grinned as others whirled around, spotted the news crew, and burst into excited conversation. As they'd spread the word about the treasure hunt, both in person and online, Hannah and her coconspirators had kept that part quiet. Hailey wanted the crowd to be as organic as possible, not filled with people who just wanted to be part of a news story or dressed to impress rather than to go tromping across the countryside.

The van stopped halfway down the street, its door swinging open before the wheels had even come to a halt. Hailey jumped out, a microphone already in hand and as polished as ever, despite the very sensible boots on her feet. She waved to Hannah and Lacy, calling, "Everybody just keep doing what you're doing for a minute while I record my intro."

A cameraman emerged with a massive camera on his shoulder. Another woman followed, draped in what Hannah assumed was sound equipment. They'd clearly been gearing up on the drive, given their tardiness.

Hannah gave the crew a thumbs-up and shouted to the crowd, "Stop staring at the camera, everyone. Face me as if I'm giving you instructions. Which I'll do momentarily."

Jim Comstock raised his hand. "Question. Why did you call a news crew for what could well be a disappointment? I mean, *I* was convinced by the clues you laid out, but just because you found the place the story was talking about doesn't mean there's actually anything buried there. It's a novel, not a documentary."

Hannah had been grinning so much this morning that her cheeks were beginning to hurt. "Trust us. There's something there."

A murmur went up from the crowd. "No offense, Hannah, but unless you're the author, you can't know that." Alice's eyes narrowed. "You're not, are you? No, you couldn't be. You didn't even know who Pru Tyler was. Unless you were faking that."

"I wasn't faking, and I'm not the author." Hannah lifted her hands, palms out. "But the author has been in touch. He's the one who assured me that anyone who goes on this hunt is going to find a treasure."

"You know who it is?" someone else asked.

"Did you get an email from the author, like that bookseller at the festival?" Liam asked from where he stood beside Archer.

Wyatt *had* been emailing her all week, and the assurance he'd asked her to pass along had come through one such message. "Yes, B.B. has been emailing me and Lacy."

"Why you?" John asked. Then he waved his hand. "I don't mean that in a bad way. But the bookseller made perfect sense. Why did B.B. pick you two to spearhead this instead of, say, Josh Hanes here, since we're starting at his house, or Wyatt or Tracy, since they were the ones set on getting the whole town on board with all the stuff for the tourists?"

Wyatt had stationed himself at the back of the crowd, no doubt to keep his finger on the pulse of public favor—or lack thereof. "Maybe B.B. was at the festival and saw Hannah and Lacy with Hailey Cassidy," he said. "If he wanted media coverage, they'd have looked like the perfect contacts."

More chatter erupted as people discussed Wyatt's point. Hannah exchanged a smile with Lacy, glad Wyatt had fielded that one. She'd received a few other such questions through the week and had done her best to sidestep them without saying anything untrue.

But it was a bit like a surprise party. Sometimes creative information was required to get people to show up, but it wasn't with the intention of deceiving them. Especially since Wyatt had finally agreed to reveal at the treasure site that he was the author. She knew he'd been wrestling with the decision all week and suspected Sandy had been the one to finally convince him. Not for his sake, but for Annabeth's.

She deserves for everyone to know how talented she was, he'd written in his final email yesterday. *Sandy's right about that. And that will be especially true after we dig up this box. This isn't about me, as I've been realizing this week. If people are still mad, I'm sorry about that. I hope they won't be. But if so, they can come to me about it and maybe have a conversation. I think, sometimes, that's all people really need.*

From the corner of her eye, Hannah spotted the cameraman giving Hailey a countdown. Her back was to the crowd so that they'd be in the shot behind her, and Hannah had no hope of hearing what she said. But she looked forward to watching the footage later in the week. Hailey had said it would probably air on Friday, to give production time to edit it and take advantage of one of their better-rated days.

It only took Hailey a minute or so to record her intro. Then she turned to the crowd and waved for Hannah and Lacy to begin.

"Okay, everyone!" Lacy shouted. "Neil's going to pass out copies of the map."

Neil grabbed a stack of them from the box he'd carried onto the porch and hurried into the crowd to distribute them.

Hannah took over. "Couple rules here. This isn't a race. B.B. was clear that he wanted this to be a group endeavor. There are too many of us to stay completely together, and I know people walk at different speeds, but as you fall into smaller groups, don't think that if you're a little slower than the group in front of you, you're going to miss out. Whoever arrives at each new stop along the way will wait for the others before the next clue is read out. And whoever gets to the final site first will wait for everyone else to arrive before we start digging."

"We've already recruited our emergency personnel to do the manual labor." Lacy motioned to Liam and Archer, who stood with the two sheriff's deputies, twins Alex and Jacky Holt. Jacky hoisted her shovel as if it were a championship trophy.

"Are we ready?"

A chorus of affirmatives rang out, so Hannah pulled out the list of clues Wyatt had planted in the book. "Okay. We all know that in the novel, the mystery started here at the old Buchanan house. The schoolmarm, Miss Temple, was out for an evening walk when she witnessed the burial of the money that ultimately got her killed. According to the fictional Mrs. Buchanan, she'd seen Miss Temple walk south down the street and take a left toward the Five and Dime. Anyone know what building used to house the Five and Dime? That's where our next clue will be."

It was fun to see the younger members of the crowd turn to their elders, eyes alight with excitement. And just as fun to hear the older neighbors bickering good-naturedly over it.

"That's where the dollar store is now."

"No, no, it's the drugstore."

"Pretty sure it's Blackberry Market."

Lacy linked their arms together. "We better lead the way."

"Let's go." They all but skipped from the Haneses' porch toward the heart of the historical district.

They'd already let everyone know that the group would be walking a total of about a mile, first in town and then to a field outside it, and that there'd be several stops along the way for clue-deciphering. Still, Hannah cast an eye over the crowd to make sure everyone there was capable of the walk. Of course, Liam, Archer, Jacky, and Alex had already taken up the rear so that they would arrive at the digging site last. It would ensure that no one missed the reveal, and they'd be able to assist anyone who fell behind.

Hailey intercepted as they struck out toward Main Street, her cameraman walking backward at a steady clip, lens trained on them. "I'm here now with local restaurateur Hannah Prentiss and Bluegrass Hollow Farm owner Lacy Minyard. You're both from families with deep roots in Blackberry Valley, correct?"

Hannah smiled, having already been prepped with the questions Hailey planned to ask. "That's right, Hailey. The Prentiss family has been in this town since shortly after its founding, and my great-grandmother, Hannah Jane Prentiss, was mentioned in *Blackberry Secrets*. The cookie jar scene inspired me to create a new display for my restaurant. The Hot Spot currently has Hannah Jane Prentiss's Cookie Jar, full of fresh-baked cookies from my great-grandmother's recipes. Like all of our menu, it's seasonal, so make sure you don't miss them."

"And they are delicious," Hailey said for the camera, "as I can personally attest. Lacy, did anyone from your family show up in the book?"

"They did, yes. I come from the Johnston family, who have been farming our land since around 1890. In *Blackberry Secrets*, Max is actually hired by a Johnston to help with the spring planting, and it's while he's working in our fields that he realizes a very crucial detail about the villain—though I won't spoil it for those who haven't read the book." Lacy flashed Hailey a smile.

"When the two of you realized that you could follow the clues in the book to a real-life prize, why did you decide to rally the whole community to search for it instead of going on the hunt by yourselves?" Hailey asked.

Lacy answered first this time, per their agreement as they'd reviewed the questions together. "I think one of the most beautiful things about *Blackberry Secrets*, and what may be a big part of its instant success, is that it so accurately captures the feel of our small-town community. The people have flaws and faults and shortcomings, but they also know the value of helping one another, working together, and giving of themselves for the sake of their neighbors."

"Exactly." Hannah gestured at the crowd behind her. "I think the author chose to use the real names of past Blackberry Valley residents as a way to honor our legacy, so we knew he'd want us to do the same with this treasure hunt. Come together as a community to discover whatever he has in store for us."

Hailey quirked a brow. "So you think that this treasure was planted by the author recently, not left there undiscovered for generations?"

"We're certain of it," Lacy said. "B.B. Smith has been in communication with us and has admitted as much."

"But that doesn't make it any less fun." They'd reached the corner and turned onto Main Street as they talked, and now Hannah motioned toward the facade of the grocery store. "And here we are, at the location of our second clue."

"I'll leave you ladies to your guide duties." Hailey gestured for her cameraman to cut filming and then turned to them with a grin. "Perfect. I'm going to hang back with the other groups and do some quick interviews as you move on to the next stop, but I'll catch up with you guys at the end. Don't start shoveling without me."

"Promise." Hannah shifted to be near the store's front door without blocking the entrance.

Once everyone had gathered again, Lacy laid out the second clue, which would lead them to the edge of town.

They followed the same pattern for the next forty minutes, smiling at how everyone laughed and joked even as they argued about how to interpret each clue. Hannah was touched by how they'd split into groups. They hadn't broken up according to who walked faster versus slower, as she'd expected, but rather with the younger or stronger pairing up with relatives or friends who might need an extra hand now and then. The elder members of the groups were more likely to know the history of the clues, and she caught snippets of conversation that proved it. The younger ones had started asking questions that had nothing to do with the treasure hunt at all, and the conversation was rich and flowing.

By the time they arrived at the slice of Granger property where Wyatt had buried the mysterious treasure, the sun was warm enough that Hannah was glad they'd thought ahead and hauled coolers full of beverages to the site earlier that morning, along with some snacks. Her neighbors must have been glad of it too, because everyone sounded quite happy to spot the refreshments.

Dad moved back to Hannah's side as she helped herself to a drink, a bottle of cold water already in his hand and a bright smile on his face. "Did you do this?" He motioned toward the folding table they'd set up.

"Lacy and I set it all up this morning. We figured it would be pretty warm by this time of day, and that everyone would have worked up a sweat on the walk."

He gave her a quick squeeze. "Always so thoughtful."

She flushed at the compliment. "I just want everyone to have a great day. And taste one of Hannah Jane's cookies."

"I think you've been successful there. Ah, there's the digging crew."

Even if Dad hadn't pointed them out, Hannah wouldn't have been able to miss them for long. They held the shovel over their heads while the crowd cheered their arrival. They stopped under the oak tree, and Liam called to Hannah, "Where shall I dig, O fearless leader?"

"Oh, I know this part!" Alice pulled away from Jules and jogged forward, her face bright and clear. "Max's probe hit metal around a root that resembled a hand, right in front of the thumb. Let's see."

She studied the massive, gnarled roots of the tree, walking around it until she found what she was searching for. "Over here, Chief."

Liam followed her and started digging where she pointed.

Even knowing for a fact there was something there, Hannah wasn't immune to the anticipation the filled the air. When Lacy came up beside her, she grabbed her best friend's hand. "What do you think will be in the box?" she asked quietly.

"More of Hannah Jane's cookies," Lacy said with a grin. "I have no idea, honestly. But we'll soon find out."

Liam must not have started digging in exactly the right spot. A few minutes went by with only the soft chatter of the crowd, which had fanned out into a circle to watch him, and the sound of shovelfuls of dirt hitting the ground. "How deep should I go, Hannah?" he called.

"Not very. If you're not finding it right there, you'll probably need to adjust where you're digging."

"Aye, aye." A couple more minutes of digging and then came the sound of his shovel hitting metal.

A cheer went up from the crowd, and everyone, Hannah included, pressed forward to watch as Liam finished uncovering the box and tugged it free of the earth.

Wyatt emerged from the group he'd been standing with and moved into place beside Liam. He held up his hands for silence and waited until it had come before drawing in a deep breath. "I want to thank you all for coming out today," he said, voice projecting over the group and no doubt straight to the camera rolling at the back of the gathering. "And I want to tell you a little story about my grandmother."

Chapter Twenty-One

Blackberry Valley
June 20, 1936

Annabeth smoothed a hand over the delicate fabric of her dress, turning to see herself in Sammy's full-length mirror. She scarcely recognized the young woman smiling back at her. Her hair, usually a boring middling brown that she kept in a bun so it was out of her face while she worked, had been curled and brushed into gleaming chestnut waves that fell to her shoulders. Sammy had chosen a dress for her that matched her blue eyes, far nicer than anything else she'd ever worn. She'd even lent her jewelry to complement it, so gold winked at her ears and throat.

"You are gorgeous," Sammy said, coming up beside her on one side while Pru took her place on the other. Together, the three of them reminded Annabeth of a summertime bouquet with their dresses of blue, green, and pink. "You both are."

"I think you mean we *all* are." Pru wrapped an arm around Annabeth's waist. "I'm glad you finally agreed to come to this, Annie."

Sammy had invited Annabeth to her family's annual summer party for the last five years, since they'd been old enough to attend the dinner and dance that would spill from the mansion's ballroom out into the gardens, but she'd always felt like she shouldn't come. That she wouldn't belong.

This year, however, she'd given up arguing when Edwin asked her if she'd "grant him the honor of escorting her" to the town's biggest social event of the season. She'd said yes. And then had little choice but to let Sammy lend her a dress, because she certainly didn't own anything suitable for the occasion.

It had been fun to spend the day getting ready with Sammy and Pru. They'd painted their nails, taken forever to get one another's hair just right, tried on half of the Adamses' jewelry collection before deciding on the right pieces, and then finally zipped and buttoned themselves into their party dresses.

"We could pass for movie stars." Sammy struck a dramatic pose.

Annabeth laughed along with Pru. "Wait until Ben Cassidy gets a load of you."

Sammy's blush nearly matched her pink dress. She'd finally relented and let her mother invite the pastor for dinner a month ago. Before the evening was over, Ben and Sammy were taking a stroll together through the gardens and realizing how much they had in common. They'd been all but inseparable since.

A knock sounded on the door, and Mrs. Adams stepped in, her smile soft and affectionate as she took them in. "You're all stunning. And your gentlemen have all arrived. They're waiting downstairs, if you're ready."

Annabeth reached for her friends' hands and gave them a squeeze. She and Edwin had gone to the soda shop a few times, and he'd taken to walking her home most evenings, but today would mark the first time they'd done anything so formal, so public. At an event where his parents would be too.

His mother had returned from Louisville on Monday, but Annabeth hadn't seen her yet. The thought of doing so tonight, when Annabeth was there as Edwin's date, formed knots in her stomach.

Sammy used their joined hands to tug them away from the mirror and toward the door. "We're ready, Mama."

Annabeth wasn't so sure she was ready, but since cowering in her best friend's bedroom all night wasn't really an option, she dragged in a deep breath and let her friends lead her into the hallway. They followed Mrs. Adams down the stairs.

A string quartet was already set up in the ballroom, and their sweet music drifted up to greet the girls. It soothed her nerves a little. Until she saw Ben

Cassidy, Joseph Grant, and Edwin Buchanan all standing together, handsome in their black suits, laughing like old friends even though neither Ben nor Edwin had grown up in Blackberry Valley. Seeing them made the butterflies flutter in Annabeth's middle again.

Edwin raised his head, and their gazes locked. The nerves melted away as he smiled. She still wasn't sure why he'd set his sights on her, not really. Why he continued to gaze at her as if she were a princess rather than a pauper. Why he sought her opinions and made it clear he valued them. Why he moved now to intercept her as if he couldn't wait to enter the ballroom with her on his arm.

His fingers felt warm and strong as they enveloped hers. His eyes gleamed. "You take my breath away," he whispered.

The heat in her cheeks told her that they probably matched Sammy's pink dress. "You clean up rather nicely yourself, Mr. Buchanan."

He chuckled and tucked her hand into his elbow. "Will you dance with me?"

She'd learned how to dance from Sammy years before, but she'd never imagined that she'd get the chance to use the lessons. "I'd be delighted."

As they moved into the ballroom, she noted how Pru surreptitiously approached another girl they knew from school and fixed her skirt where it was tucked up. How Mr. Prentiss handed his fresh cup of punch to

Mrs. Taylor when she coughed. How old Mr. Lumer led his nearly blind wife through the crowd and to a chair with a gentle hand on her back, and neighbors were quick to move anything that might trip her up.

Annabeth had noticed a thousand such things over the last two months. Since she'd started watching for them. None of her neighbors were perfect. They still groused and complained and bickered, like all humans. But that was never all they did. There was far more good in them than bad. She'd just been too blinded by her own insecurities and childhood wounds to see it.

The realization had changed everything. Suddenly she'd remembered the times that she'd gone to check the mail at the rusted old box and found food inside. Or envelopes heavy with coins that had always made Mother cry when she opened them and felt those precious discs. She remembered who would see her walking past their houses as a girl and call her in, offering her a sandwich if she'd help them finish weeding their gardens.

How had she gone so long without realizing that they'd been trying to help, and to spare her family's pride as they did so? Not everyone—there had been those who judged, who accused. But enough that she began to understand how she could have been more a part of this community long ago, had she been brave enough to look past her own interpretations.

Edwin led her onto the dance floor, where other couples were already doing the foxtrot. They joined in then transitioned to the cotillion. They were just finishing up a more sedate waltz when Edwin's gaze caught on something or someone behind her. He led her off the dance floor.

Her good mood faded, replaced by apprehension when she saw he was guiding her straight toward his parents.

She'd known she wouldn't be able to avoid talking to them all evening. She had assumed that Edwin would do exactly this at some point. But all the pep talks in the world couldn't prepare her for this.

So she sent a silent prayer heavenward.

Mr. Buchanan was dashing in his tuxedo, Mrs. Buchanan lovely and elegant in a dark rose silk gown. There was no evidence of the panicked, desperate woman who had chased her down Main Street at the beginning of May.

But neither did she look quite like the stern, detached woman who'd always presided over the house while Annabeth cleaned it. Maybe the time with her daughter and grandchildren had softened her.

Regardless, Mrs. Buchanan didn't scowl at her or lift her nose in disdain. In fact, when Edwin halted them at her side, she reached for Annabeth's hand. "It's so good to see you tonight, Annabeth, dear."

It was? Annabeth probably looked like a fool, blinking in surprise as she was. But she recovered quickly and offered a smile. "You too, ma'am. I hope you had a wonderful time in Louisville with your daughter. She must have felt very blessed to have you there, helping with the new baby."

Joy lit the woman's eyes. "I didn't intend to stay quite so long, but I couldn't drag myself away from those precious little ones. I took roll after roll of photographs. You'll have to join us for dinner soon, and I'll show them to you."

What exactly had Edwin told his mother to make her so welcoming? Annabeth didn't know, but the glance she sneaked at him showed only that he wore an easy smile. "I would like that very much," she assured his mother, giving her fingers a light squeeze. And she meant it.

Mrs. Buchanan wove their arms together. "Walk with me a moment, won't you? Let's go and see what desserts they have set up in the drawing room. I saw someone with a little cake that was quite tempting."

She couldn't exactly object, not when Mrs. Buchanan was already tugging her away and Edwin had merely moved aside with a wink.

They strolled out of the ballroom, past countless neighbors who greeted them both with friendly words. Every step made something in Annabeth coil tighter. Had the welcome been a show in front of her husband and son? Once she had Annabeth out of sight and someplace quieter, would Mrs. Buchanan order her to stay away from Edwin? Accuse her of conniving? Gold digging?

She feared she was right when the woman led her not toward the drawing room with its tables full of treats, but rather into the library, which was open to guests but currently empty of anyone else. Nausea churned in Annabeth's stomach.

Mrs. Buchanan halted a few feet inside and faced her. But there was no accusation on her face. On the contrary, she appeared contrite. Her blue eyes were glassy with unshed tears as she caught Annabeth's hands and whispered, "I do hope you'll forgive me for the horrid things I said to you that day. I have no excuse to offer you. Just the assurance that I know I was in the wrong, and that I have regretted my actions and words every day since."

Annabeth let out her pent-up breath, and her stomach settled along with the exhale. "Of course I forgive you."

"I don't know why you would." Mrs. Buchanan blinked, and the tears spilled over her cheeks. "I know Edwin told you the truth about me. And he told me how gracious you have been to keep our secret and how faithful you've been to pray for me since learning it."

"It has been a blessing to pray for you." Annabeth shifted their hands so that she could grip Mrs. Buchanan's and give them an encouraging squeeze. "Everyone has their struggles, but no one should have to bear them alone."

The woman reclaimed one of her hands to wipe at her cheeks. "I have felt so alone. Henry and Edwin love me, but they don't understand. How can they, when I don't understand myself? Fortunately, my daughter found a pastor in Louisville for me to talk to. Someone who has struggled with the same thing. That was another reason I stayed so long. I met with him and his wife twice a week for the last month, and they helped me learn new ways to fight these compulsions when they come upon me. I intend to visit again in September and check in with them, and I'm to write to them in the meantime."

"I'm so glad to hear that." Annabeth could pray for her, and she could even empathize with the desperation, but she certainly had no practical advice to offer. She was grateful that someone else did. "And I know Edwin and your husband must be too."

She nodded, ducking her head a bit. It must be difficult for such a proud woman to admit that she needed help. Realizing anew what she'd put her family through. What strength of character it took to commit herself to change in such a vulnerable way.

"I wanted to say too, while I have you here, that I'm truly glad that Edwin is courting you. I know I didn't react well when I first saw his interest, but that was my fear and prejudice speaking. Edwin copied out and mailed me that little story you'd written for him, and I could see at once why he's so smitten. You're so clever and intelligent, and I could see your heart in your words. Your goodness. I'm sorry it took that for me to see it, when I could have seen it for myself if I'd simply paid attention when you were at my house."

Annabeth's cheeks went hot again. Edwin had asked if he could share the story, but she'd thought he'd meant with a friend. She never dreamed he'd mail a copy to his mother. "You're too kind. It was just a silly little story."

"It wasn't. It was a story layered with depth and mercy and grace. Things that touched me deeply, because I had become sorely aware of how much I need them." Mrs. Buchanan cupped Annabeth's cheek in the very way her own mother used to. She peered into her eyes with open affection and faith. "You're going to be good for my son, and I say as a biased mother that I dare to think he'll be good for you too. I've never seen him so happy, so confident and sure of himself. He's blessed to have found you."

Soft laughter slipped from Annabeth's lips. "I'm the one who's blessed."

The woman's smile widened. "Happily, blessings go both ways." She nodded toward the doorway. "Now let's go find those desserts."

Chapter Twenty-Two

Hannah found herself holding her breath and praying for wisdom for Wyatt as he stood in front of the group of townspeople. No doubt he saw, as she did, the questions on many of their faces as he thanked them for coming. Why was *he* thanking them? Why did he want to tell them about his grandmother?

This must be hard for him. He'd gone to such lengths to preserve his anonymity, and that would be hard to give up, especially after so many people had reacted to the book with outrage. But she believed he was doing the right thing in admitting his authorship. Especially, as he'd said, because it meant truly giving his grandmother credit for her part in the story.

Wyatt paused, glanced at Sandy as if for emotional support, and then cleared his throat. "Some of you probably remember her—Annabeth Billings Buchanan. She and my grandfather lived here into the '80s, when they both passed away. Those of you who were around back then probably remember that they were always quick to help those in need, whether it was with an encouraging word or a literal helping hand. What most of you probably don't realize is that Gran was a writer. She had some things published in magazines, but she never made a big fuss or told anyone about it. Mostly, she wrote for her own therapy, as she called it. To process her world and get her thoughts and feelings out. When I was a kid, though, she let me read a novel she'd written in her early twenties. It was called *Blackberry Secrets*."

There it was—the swell of voices expressing their surprise and confusion. For a moment, it was general chaos, but eventually Alice's voice rose above the din. "You're telling us that novel was written almost a hundred years ago, at the time when it was set?"

Wyatt nodded. "Mostly, yes. I rewrote it to sound more in line with what readers expect from books today, but it was her plot, her characters, her insights into everyone. She said if ever she published it, she meant to change all the names." He shrugged, looking sheepish. "I thought you all would get a kick out of seeing your ancestors in those pages, like I did. Max was based on her father, you see. A man I never got to meet but still felt like I got to know through her book. I hoped you would all feel the same. For those of you who didn't, I am truly sorry. I hope you know that. I never intended the book to bring you anything but joy."

Hannah studied the crowd to gauge everyone's reactions. Those who had already embraced the book were smiling, nodding. Those who'd been upset by it were softening, most of them turning to a neighbor to say something with rueful smiles on their faces. Perhaps pausing to realize that the story had done far more than expose old skeletons. It had fleshed them out into real people that they should all be proud to have come from.

"So, what about the treasure?" someone shouted from the rear of the group.

Wyatt laughed. "That part was fictionalized. But I wanted to give something back to you all, so I planned from the get-go to really plant something to be found here." He motioned to Liam, who had put the box on a table they'd set up next to the ones holding refreshments. He held out a small silver key. "Chief, would you do the honors?"

Liam took the key, inserted it into the lock, and opened the lid with a metallic creak.

Hannah leaned forward like everyone else, vying for a glimpse of what was inside.

Liam's brows furrowed. He pulled out a few envelopes and held them aloft. "We've got quite a few envelopes in here. Each one has a family name on it."

"My suggestion," Wyatt said, "is that you all gather with your families to open your envelope. Of course, some of you will hail from multiple families, so don't be afraid to mingle afterward and visit your cousins or friends and share."

Hannah strained to see where Dad and Uncle Gordon had gotten to. When she spotted them, she had to do some fancy footwork to avoid colliding with other people making similar dashes toward family members.

She'd just reached them when Liam came around with some of the envelopes in his hand. He smiled and handed her the one with *Prentiss* written on it then moved off to another group. Wyatt and Sandy had taken some of the envelopes as well and were weaving through the crowd to pass them out.

The envelope was clearly new, its paper white and crisp, but when she slid her finger under the flap and broke the seal, the paper that peeked out was a different story. It wasn't quite yellow but wasn't quite white, and when she pulled it out and unfolded the pages, she saw it was watermarked with the logo for a nearby paper mill that had been shut down decades ago.

Her dad and uncle read over her shoulders as she smoothed out the creases, revealing typewritten paragraphs formatted like a letter and clearly pounded out on a typewriter, not printed from a computer.

That became all the more obvious when she saw the date at the top.

September 23, 1954

Dear Hannah Jane and Mark,

I saw what you did today. You didn't know I was there, didn't think anyone was watching. And I'll let you go on thinking it. But I saw.

I saw the look you exchanged when that barefoot boy came up to you as you sat in your backyard. I saw the way your knuckles went white on the arm of your chair, Hannah Jane, when he asked if you had any odd jobs he could do. I saw the despairing look you cast around, Mark, at the yard you'd just spent the whole day mowing and raking and pruning. I saw the sweat on your brow, still gleaming in the sun.

You could have said no and turned him away. Some people would have. You could have even snapped that had he shown up a couple hours earlier, he could have helped you out, but he was too late.

But you didn't do that. And as I saw the two of you exchange glances, I had a feeling you were hearing the words our pastor said a few weeks ago, when he was preaching on the parable of the landowner who went out all those many times to bring in workers. I imagined you were hearing him remind us that with the Lord, there's no such thing as too late. That with the Lord, all who are willing to follow Him into the fields will receive His grace, His mercy, and His reward.

I wasn't surprised when you stood up, Hannah Jane, and pulled around another chair at your little patio table for the boy, nor when you invited him to sit down while you made a list of things he could do. I certainly wasn't surprised when you asked him if he liked cookies and milk and went to bring out a glass and the whole cookie jar for him to choose his own.

I smiled when I saw that jar. You know why. And I know well you did indeed count the cookies he ended up pulling out. Five? Six? I couldn't quite see from where I sat on Jenny's back porch, peeking between the tree limbs and the slatted fence at your yard, but I know he took quite a few, and I know you counted only so that you could gauge how hungry he was.

I know for a fact you weren't hungry, Mark, because you'd just finished supper. But you said you were, and you went inside and made sandwiches, so you could share one with that boy without him thinking you were doing it for him.

Did you see him fold that last half of the sandwich into his napkin and put it in his pocket? I suspect you did. But you didn't call him out on it. No, you weren't going to offend his pride or make him feel like you were interrogating him. But I wondered, as I suspect you did, if he was saving it for later—or taking it to someone else.

I wonder, too, at the things you put on that list of yours, Hannah Jane. Were they real chores that needed to be done—maybe some of the ones I used to do for you back in the day?

Or did you write down any old thing that came to mind and would bring that child back to your house another day, so you could push more food and money into his hands? Either way, I know how your heart would have ached as you turned that list over to him and saw him struggle to read it.

You didn't question his lack of ability, despite the fact that he was old enough to know how. No, you did that thing I've seen you do so many times. You blamed yourself, claiming your handwriting was atrocious and apologizing for expecting him to read it. And you leaned in close and ran your finger under your "sloppy" words and showed him what they said.

You didn't just read them to him. You ensured that he didn't feel bad for not knowing how. You did something better. You did the sort of thing you always do.

Mark, I saw you try to follow him when he finally left with a promise to return the next day to help out, but given the slump to your shoulders when you returned twenty minutes later, he gave you the slip. I pray you don't let it weigh you down too much, though I know it will. Because I think that boy will be back. I think you'll have plenty of chances to earn his trust and figure out where he's holing up. I know you'll do everything you can to help him, whatever that means.

You didn't see me watching as I sat on Jenny's porch, shelling that mess of peas for her. But I saw you, my friends. I saw those hearts I've come to love so dearly reminding me of why I've come to love them so dearly. And I know our Lord saw it too. I know He has a great reward in store for you.

Because it wasn't just that boy you served today. It was Jesus Himself. And someday, He's going to draw you both into His embrace and say, "Well done, good and faithful servants."

I won't embarrass you by saying it out loud. But I'm thinking it, cheering it too. Well done, my good and faithful friends. Well done.

Annabeth

Hannah wiped at her cheeks when she felt the tickle of tears on them, sniffing and pushing the paper into her dad's hands so she could reach into her pocket for a tissue and do a better job of mopping up her emotions.

Dad cleared his throat too and blinked rapidly a few times. "Wow. That was our grandparents. Always finding ways to help, but rarely letting anyone know they were doing it. Such good people. Such good, good people."

"She could be prickly, and he could be stern." Uncle Gordon took the pages from her dad with a smile. "But we always joked that it was a cover. That they were marshmallows inside. Soft and sweet."

"I wish you'd had a chance to know them better, Hannah," Dad said. "Like we did. Like this Annabeth did."

"I wish I had too," she admitted, tucking her tissue back into her pocket. "But I feel like I do now, in a way. This letter, the bits of her I saw in the novel—they were a first-person account that helped me feel closer to both of them. What a gift."

"You think that's what all those envelopes are?" Uncle Gordon looked around, though with everyone clustered around their respective gifts, there was no way to see what each envelope contained.

"Letters that Annabeth wrote to her friends and neighbors but never gave them?"

Wyatt must have heard the question. He joined them, contentment in every line of his face. "Snapshots of kindness. That's what she always called them," he said. "Except that she took snapshots with words, not photographs. I found them when I was young and couldn't figure out why she had all those letters to people that she'd never mailed. But she told me those people had been following Jesus's commands to do good in private. She never wanted to call out those quiet acts of kindness and embarrass them. But she wanted to remember each small deed. So she wrote them down and kept them."

"That's so beautiful." Hannah gazed out across the gathering, seeing other people wiping at their eyes, laughing together, trading letters with cousins and friends. "Makes me wonder how many small acts of love I haven't noticed."

"Same here," Wyatt agreed. "I think it's something we have to train ourselves to take time to notice. Most of the time we're so busy with our own lives that we don't really pause to see those moments in others'. But they're there."

They were. She knew they were, and she vowed to notice more of them. To appreciate the ones she saw. To do more such small acts, every moment she could. Not because anyone like Annabeth was watching, but because the Lord was.

Though maybe it mattered that others might be too, even when she didn't know it. Because even that was encouraging. Sometimes, all it took to renew one's faith was to see someone else acting in God's love.

Wasn't that part of what community was all about—edifying and encouraging one another, even when no one else noticed?

Lacy approached their group with overbright eyes and the Johnston envelope in hand. "Trade?"

"You bet." Uncle Gordon handed her the Prentiss one and started reading hers.

Hannah didn't immediately look down at the page though. She was too busy tracking Alice as she wove her way through the crowd, searching for someone. Wyatt, apparently, because when she finally spotted him, she moved faster than Hannah had ever seen her go before. Marched straight up to him and threw her arms around him.

Wyatt laughed and held her tight. "My grandmother sure loved Pru," he said.

Alice tightened her hold, her eyes squeezed shut. "I was so put out that you didn't have more of the Tylers in that book of yours. But I see now. She didn't include the people she knew and loved best—she had nothing to work through with them. But she still saw them. Loved them so dearly. I'm going to treasure that letter forever."

"That was my hope for everyone." They pulled away, and Wyatt laughed. "I know it's not gold or silver, but—"

"No. It's better than that." Alice patted his arm and gave a decisive nod. "You gave us a new appreciation for our family. And that's the most precious thing in the world."

Hannah was glad Hailey was recording all of this. She patted her pockets for her phone, wanting a few photos, but it wasn't in her shorts. She hadn't brought a bag. Looking around, she spotted her distinctive case on the edge of the food table, where she must have set it down when she'd opened a cooler for some water.

When she picked it up and unlocked the screen, she had to laugh. Her contact for Liam was there. He'd changed his name to Liam *"Treasure Hunter" Berthold*. Spinning around, she saw him standing with some of his cousins, watching her. He winked. She lifted her phone and took a photo of the group. Then turned to take more of all her neighbors.

"You're not trying to scoop me, are you?" Hailey came up from behind her with a grin and motioned to her phone. "Planning to send those to a rival news outlet?"

Hannah laughed. "Not at all. I'm starting my own snapshots of kindness."

"A likely story." Hailey tilted her head. "Hey, that's not a bad headline for this. What do you think?"

"I love it."

"I'd better write it down before I forget." Hailey took out her own phone and tapped at the screen, apparently making a digital note for herself. "The guys want to get back to the van to start uploading this here in a few, but I'll catch you at the open house."

"You're staying for that?"

"You think I'd miss a chance to see that house?" Hailey grinned. "But we promised to leave the cameras in the van. We'll be there solely as guests."

Hannah could imagine the cameras would be a bit too much for Claire. "Great. I'll see you there."

She joined her family and Lacy once more, finally reading Annabeth's letter to the Johnstons, which was every bit as touching as the one she had written to Hannah Jane and Mark. "Heartwarming, isn't it?" she said to Lacy.

Her best friend smiled. "More than that. It's inspiring. Makes me want to live my life in a way that's worthy of such a legacy."

Hannah thought for a moment, and a smile tugged at her lips. "You know, I think that's exactly what a good story's meant to do."

From the Author

Dear Reader,

The power of story is a theme I've given a lot of thought to over the years and have explored in various ways in several books I've written. I knew it would be especially fun to have a story that was clearly more than *just* a story, and venture into the things that were possible when the lines between fact and fiction were as blurred as they were in *Blackberry Secrets*. I also loved the chance to explore the importance of family and the legacies that get passed down from one generation to the next, sometimes good and sometimes bad.

I hope that you enjoyed the stories I chose to tell, both the one Hannah discovered and the one she lived out as she hunted for the author's true identity. Mostly, I hope we can all be reminded of the importance of both grieving and rejoicing together, of looking for the goodness in others, and of opening ourselves up with vulnerability, giving our friends and neighbors the opportunity to bless us with their love too.

As I wrote this book, I was going through chemotherapy for breast cancer. In a lot of ways, it has been humbling to be the one to need help, to learn to receive when I much prefer to give. But oh, the blessings God poured out to me through His people. As my mailbox was flooded with cards, letters, and gifts from people all over the country, I was continually amazed at how thoughtful, kind, and generous the Church really is. I wanted to capture a bit of that in this book. I pray it brings you just a sliver of the joy I've felt throughout this journey.

Signed,
Roseanna

About the Author

Roseanna M. White is a bestselling, Christy Award-winning author who has long claimed that words are the air she breathes. When not writing fiction, she's homeschooling, editing, designing book covers, and pretending her house will clean itself. Roseanna is the author of a slew of historical novels that span several continents and thousands of years. Spies and war and mayhem always seem to find their way into her books...to offset her real life, which is blessedly ordinary.

The Hot Spotlight

Kentucky's Apple Festivals

The Apple Festival featured in *A Likely Story* may have been fictional, but it was a mash-up of several regional festivals that Kentucky towns sponsor each fall. Many of the festivals have been going on for decades, and in those years, they've grown and evolved into events designed to bring joy to modern attendees.

Some of the real-life festivals feature pageants that crown Apple Princes and Princesses that reign over the event, contests and games for children, and endless crafts. I particularly enjoyed reading about one town's quest to make the World's Largest Apple Pie at the Casey County Apple Festival. In 2023, this enormous apple pie required fifty bushels of Granny Smith apples, one hundred fifty pounds of sugar, one and a half pounds of cinnamon, seventy-five pounds of corn starch, fifteen pounds of butter, one and a half pounds of salt, and three hundred pounds of pastry for the crusts. It took twelve hours to bake this monstrous treat!

Whether they're in it for the live music, the petting zoos, the apple cider, or the baked goods, festivalgoers who attend any of these events know they're in for hours of fun, treats, and fellowship with their communities.

From the Hot Spot Kitchen

APPLE CIDER SNICKERDOODLES

Ingredients:

For the Dough:

- 8 tablespoons butter, softened
- ¾ cup granulated sugar
- 2 tablespoons cider, boiled and cooled to room temperature
- 1 large egg
- 1 teaspoon vanilla extract
- 1½ cups all-purpose flour
- 1¼ teaspoons Apple Pie Spice (see below)
- 1 teaspoon baking powder
- ½ teaspoon salt

For the Coating:

- 3 tablespoons granulated sugar
- 1 teaspoon Apple Pie Spice (see below)

Apple Pie Spice:

- 1 teaspoon cinnamon
- ¾ teaspoon nutmeg
- ½ teaspoon allspice

Directions:
1. Boil apple cider and set aside to cool. Combine Apple Pie Spice ingredients, which will be divided for use in the recipe.
2. In large bowl, beat butter and sugar until light and fluffy, about 3 to 5 minutes.
3. Beat in cider, egg, and vanilla until combined. Scrape bowl with spatula.
4. In separate bowl or measuring cup, whisk together flour, 1¼ teaspoons Apple Pie Spice, baking powder, and salt.
5. Add dry ingredients to wet, stirring until just combined with no streaks.
6. Transfer to smaller bowl, cover, and chill for at least four hours.
7. Preheat oven to 375 degrees Fahrenheit. Line two baking sheets with parchment paper or silicone baking mat.
8. Make coating by mixing sugar and remaining Apple Pie Spice in small bowl.
9. Scoop dough into 2-tablespoon-size portions and roll into balls. Drop each ball in coating mixture and roll to cover. Place balls onto cookie sheets, leaving 2 inches between them.
10. Bake 12 to 15 minutes, rotating and swapping positions of pans halfway through to ensure even baking. The cookies should be golden and set on the edges with centers still soft. Remove from oven and let cool completely on baking sheet. Store at room temperature.

Read on for a sneak peek of another exciting book in the *Mysteries of Blackberry Valley* series!

Out of the Depths
BY BETH ADAMS

Hannah Prentiss was peeling a butternut squash in the kitchen of the Hot Spot when her phone rang from her pocket. Given her nearly finished progress and her messy hands, she let the call go to voice mail.

But when it immediately rang again, she sighed and set the squash and peeler on the cutting board. It had been a chilly October so far, and the butternut squash soup—topped with fried croutons and a drizzle of cream and olive oil—had been a big hit, but it sure did mean a lot of peeling and chopping. She still had at least half a dozen left to go.

"I'll finish this in a moment," she told Jacob Forrest, the head chef at the Hot Spot, who was busy seasoning meat for the chicken marsala special. She quickly washed and dried her hands then pulled her phone out of the back pocket of her jeans.

It was her best friend, Lacy Minyard. Lacy usually texted, so the fact that she'd called Hannah twice meant something was wrong. "Hi. What's going on?"

"Have you heard from Ryder?" It sounded like Lacy was in a car, judging by the soft clicking sound of a turn signal in the background.

"Ryder?" Hannah and her cousin were friendly, but they weren't in the habit of checking in with each other regularly. "No. Why?"

"When I was coming home from town about an hour ago, I saw his car parked at the edge of the woods, right by the path that leads to the entrance to McLeod Cave. He goes there sometimes, so I didn't think anything of it. But then a few minutes ago, I saw a fire truck, an ambulance, and a police car speeding by. They pulled into the parking area where Ryder's car was. The cave entrance is the only thing down that way, so I was afraid—well, I just wanted to see if you knew what was going on."

"No." Hannah got a sinking feeling in the pit of her stomach. Lacy lived on a farm outside of Blackberry Valley, and her land held an entrance to one of the many caves that threaded underground throughout the area. Many people, including Ryder, liked to explore that particular cave, which was said to be filled with interesting rock formations and underground rivers, but it was also notoriously dangerous.

There had been plenty of stories over the years. People sometimes got turned around inside the cave, or were trapped in a tiny space they couldn't get out of, or portions of the cave walls collapsed on people. All kinds of things had happened that led to people needing to be rescued. People had even died in the cave, including one of Hannah's relatives many years before.

Hannah and her brother, Drew, had always been forbidden from venturing inside, though it wasn't exactly a temptation for Hannah, who could never get past the claustrophobia she felt in small spaces. Add to that the danger and the possibility of creepy-crawlies, and she had no interest. But Ryder, for reasons Hannah would never understand, was an active spelunker who spent a lot of time exploring and mapping the caverns around the area. Had he been exploring and gotten into trouble at last?

"It can't be good, can it?" Hannah asked. A fleet of emergency rescue vehicles wouldn't be rushing to the cave entrance unless something bad had happened.

"I'm headed there now," Lacy said. "I'll be there in a second. I can let you know what I find out."

"I'm on my way." If something terrible had happened to Ryder, Hannah wanted to hear it firsthand. "I'll see you in a few minutes." She hung up and started to untie her apron. "Will you be okay if I run out for a moment?" she asked Jacob.

"I'll be fine. It's all under control."

Hannah was grateful to have such a capable chef at the helm. He would have to peel and chop the squash himself, but he could handle that and more.

She pulled her apron over her head and hung it up, grabbed her purse, and hurried out through the dining room of the old firehouse she'd transformed into a farm-to-table restaurant.

"I'm running out for a bit," she called to Raquel Holden, one of her servers, who was sliding the printout with the night's specials into the table tents.

"No problem." Raquel barely looked up. "We'll be ready to open on time."

Dylan Bowman, Hannah's other server, was seated at one of the tables, rolling bundles of cutlery in the cloth napkins. Hannah noticed that he had two forks and no spoon in the bundle he was working on.

"Check that one again," she called before dashing out the door.

She really was lucky to have found such a capable and reliable staff. Aside from Dylan—who made more mistakes than he probably should but was likeable enough that she couldn't bring herself to replace him—she had no qualms about leaving her restaurant in their hands. Raquel and hostess Elaine Wilby would double-check Dylan's work.

Hannah hopped into her Subaru Outback and headed down Main Street, driving past the brick storefronts and cafés that lined the quaint downtown, past the old Victorian homes and lush lawns of the residential area, then out of the main part of town, where she was surrounded by open fields on both sides. Along the road, trees blazed in shades of fiery orange and red and gold, and behind the fence on the left side, chestnut-colored horses stood in the shade of a redbud tree. She would never get over how beautiful Blackberry Valley was. After years of living in California, she had returned to central Kentucky where she'd grown up and had developed a new appreciation for its beauty.

Bluegrass Hollow Farm, which Lacy's family had owned for generations, was a few miles out of town. Hannah passed Lacy and Neil's white farmhouse and kept driving. She turned onto a dirt side road and followed it along the creek until she saw the police cars and fire truck parked under a grove of trees. She parked behind Lacy's pickup and stepped out.

The first person she saw was her cousin Ryder talking to twin deputies Alex and Jacky Holt. Ryder wore tan overalls that were covered in dust and a helmet with a light on the front. He gestured wildly, though Hannah couldn't tell what he was trying to convey. Whatever it was, he was excited.

Colt Walker, a firefighter on the Blackberry Valley squad, stood next to him, also wearing dusty overalls and a helmet. Two EMTs stood in the shade beside an ambulance, looking down at their phones. She let out a breath. Ryder was okay.

"Hey." Lacy joined Hannah and gave her a hug. "He's fine, obviously."

"I'm so glad." Hannah looked around at the small crowd gathered in the shade of the redbud trees. In addition to the police deputies and the EMTs, she saw Liam Berthold, the fire chief, and another firefighter standing by the fire truck, its swirling lights casting an eerie glow over the shaded area. "But what happened?" She gestured at the emergency personnel. "Why are they all here?"

"From what I understand, Ryder and Colt found something in the cave," Lacy said. "They made it into a section that hasn't been mapped because rockfall closed it off, but they found another way in, and they saw something inside."

"What was it?"

"I don't know. No one's told me any—"

"Hannah." Ryder waved her over. "You'll never believe what we found."

Hannah pulled Lacy toward her cousin then released her and hugged Ryder.

He chuckled. "Well, hello to you too, Hannah. What's that for?"

She let him go. "When Lacy called, I thought something terrible had happened to you down there."

"No such luck." Ryder had the same dark hair and brown eyes as his dad, Hannah's uncle Gordon. He was tall, and he had always been athletic and adventurous. When he wasn't working at his job as an actuary, he was out caving, backcountry camping, ice climbing, or doing some other life-threatening sport for thrills. "But we found Uncle Chuck."

"Uncle Chuck?"

"Dad and Uncle Gabriel's uncle. The one who went missing all those years ago."

"What?" Hannah was amazed. Uncle Chuck had disappeared back when her dad and Uncle Gordon were very young. He'd gone exploring in the McLeod Cave one day, as he often did. But this time, he never came out. When rescuers went in to try to find him after his wife reported him missing, they found that one of the walls of the cave had collapsed. It was pretty clear he was trapped behind the fallen rock, but after the collapse that section of the cave was too treacherous to pass, and rescuers never managed to get to him. He'd been down there all this time.

If Ryder and Colt had found his remains, that would explain why all the emergency vehicles were there. The firemen were trained to perform tricky emergency rescues, which probably meant they'd spent plenty of time rescuing people from caves. The police were there to ensure things ran smoothly, keep the public back, and lend extra hands where necessary. The paramedics would provide first aid to any crew or bystanders. Though Hannah wasn't sure what good emergency rescue or the paramedics could do for Uncle Chuck at this point. He'd been down there for decades.

"Well, not *him* exactly," Ryder said. "But proof that he was there at some point. We found his things. Hannah, he didn't die in that cave after all!" Ryder was talking so fast and with so much excitement, Hannah was having trouble following.

"How do you know that?"

"We found some things that appear to have been left in the cave by your great-uncle," Colt said. "Some things that it seems might've been left on purpose when he disappeared."

"He didn't die down there, Hannah," Ryder insisted. "I mean, all our lives, we've been told the caves aren't safe because our dads' uncle died in one. Can you imagine how surprised Dad and Uncle Gabriel are going to be? Great-Aunt Minnie is gone, of course, but Nana will be so happy to find out after all this time that her brother didn't die in the cave after all."

She could understand why Ryder was so excited. "What exactly did you find?"

"We found his things in a neat stack, just sitting there," Ryder said. "We found clothes along with his wallet, a note, a map, and a receipt."

"But if you found his things, doesn't that mean he was there but *didn't* make it out?" Hannah asked.

"No, Hannah. It wasn't like that. They weren't strewn all over. He left them on purpose." Ryder showed her a photo on his phone—clothes, papers, and a wallet in a tidy pile on the floor of a small, dark, rock-lined cavern. "See how he folded the clothes? Then there's a map, also folded, and that's his wallet with his ID inside. The receipt is for a bus ticket. He left it all there and walked away."

Hannah stared at the photo. Ryder was right. That was no haphazard pile. These weren't things left by a man trapped in a cave, clinging to life. This was a neat and deliberate pile. She couldn't believe it.

"Where are they?" She looked around for the items, wanting to examine them herself.

"Oh, they're still in the cave," Ryder said. "We left them there."

It took a moment for Hannah to absorb his words. "You did? Why?"

"We weren't sure what to do," Colt volunteered. "We didn't want to mess with the stuff, so we left it pretty much the way we found it so the police could see it, in case it's a crime scene."

"But we can lead you guys down there," Ryder said to the deputies, who stood nearby. "We can show you exactly where we found them."

"Sure," Jacky agreed. She apparently had no qualms about spelunking.

Alex scuffed the toe of his boot in the dirt and cleared his throat. "If you're telling me your uncle left his things there on purpose, then it's probably not a crime scene."

"We don't know for sure that's what he did," Colt said.

"In any case, his things are still inside the cave, and we need to see them to know for sure," Jacky said. "Which means we need to go in and get them."

"We don't all need to go," Alex said. "Maybe Ryder and Colt can go get them."

"You know as well as I do that stuff is potential evidence, which means you and I have to be the ones who handle it from now on," Jacky reminded her brother. "We're the police, remember?"

"It's getting pretty late," Alex said, gesturing at the darkening sky. The October days were certainly getting shorter, and the sun was low in the sky. "Maybe it'd be better to wait until tomorrow."

"You know it's dark inside caves, no matter what time it is, right?" Jacky laughed. "I'm tempted to keep going just to see what other excuses you come up with, but we don't have time for that." She grinned at Hannah. "My brother is claustrophobic. Makes him lots of fun for adventures like this. I'll see if Liam wants to go instead. He likes caves." She called to the fire chief and beckoned him over.

Liam headed toward the group. He wore a long-sleeved shirt and jeans, and Hannah thought how nice he looked in them. "What's up?"

"These guys found evidence relating to a missing person, but they left it inside the cave like knuckleheads."

"We thought it might be a crime scene," Ryder protested.

"I'm teasing. You did the right thing. But we need to go in and bring it out, and my brother is too scared to go." Jacky turned to Liam. "You're not afraid, are you?"

Liam shook his head. "I have a lot of experience in McLeod Cave. I don't think I've ever been in the part where you guys found evidence though. I've never seen anything like that down there."

"We'd never been there either," Ryder said. "I don't think anyone has since Uncle Chuck. The entrance he used was closed off by rockfall. That's how he got trapped in there, or so the story went. But we found a small opening coming in from the other direction and rappelled into it. It's kind of a scary descent, and I don't think most people would have tried it. I mean, obviously no one has, or they would have found that stuff."

"Definitely not doing that," Alex said.

"No problem. Let me grab my gear." Liam looked around at the gathered group. "Anyone else want to go?"

Hannah considered it, imagining Liam's strong arms guiding her down the chambers of the cave. But reality quickly set in as she remembered caves were dark, filled with narrow passages, bugs, and the potential for rockfall that could leave a person trapped underground. She'd been to several of the commercial caves in the area, with their big caverns and stairs and lights, but she knew McLeod Cave wasn't like that.

"A small opening you have to rappel down to get inside a cave is not my idea of a good time," Lacy said.

"Especially one with a 'scary descent,'" Hannah added. "No thank you."

"Suit yourself," Jacky said, shrugging. "Liam, you got an extra headlamp in that truck?"

"Caving is not for everyone," Liam said kindly. He trotted to the fire truck.

A few minutes later, Jacky and Liam sported helmets with headlamps and Liam shouldered a backpack full of gear. Hannah guessed it contained ropes and carabiners, but she really had no idea. She and Lacy followed Ryder and Colt toward the opening of the cave.

In her mind, Hannah always saw cave entrances as perfect half-ovals of rock, with the cave itself unfurling like a hallway beyond. This opening was little more than a hole in the ground, which Liam, Jacky, Colt, and Ryder descended into, using rocks as handholds and headlamps to light their way. Once they were gone, Alex went back to the police car and climbed in to wait.

Hannah knew she should leave the rest of the job to the professionals and get back to the restaurant. Saturday was their busiest night, and this was peak leaf-admiring season. With the beautiful clear skies, the Hot Spot would likely be full to bursting. Her team would need her.

But she couldn't quite make herself leave. It didn't sound like the path to Uncle Chuck's things would be an easy one, and she would worry until all four of them made it back up safely. Besides, she was too curious to leave now. Had they really found clues about what had happened to Chuck?

Hannah turned to Lacy. "You don't need to stay if you have better things to do."

"Are you kidding? There's no way I'm leaving now. I can't wait to see what they bring up." Lacy gestured toward the opening. "Besides, this is all happening on our land. I don't know what the liability issues are, but I think it makes sense for me to stay, just in case."

Hannah supposed that was true. She didn't think anyone in her family had ever blamed Lacy's family for what had happened in the cave. From what she knew, people in town were grateful that Bluegrass Hollow Farm allowed locals to access the cave entrance on their land—but she could see why Lacy was worried. Maybe they should consider limiting access to the cave or sealing up the entrance. After all, this was an age when people sued first and asked questions later.

While they waited, Hannah called Elaine to let her know she wouldn't be there in time for the first seating, but would make it to the restaurant as soon as she could. She and Lacy chatted with the remaining firefighters and paramedics who waited by their vehicles. Hannah saw Liam's best friend and fellow firefighter, Archer Lestrade.

Every few minutes, one of their walkie-talkies would squawk, but there weren't any updates from the group below.

"Is there any way to find out what's going on down there?" Hannah asked.

"Not really," Archer told her. "At least, not with what we've got here. The rocks are pretty good at absorbing radio waves, so unless they're very near the surface, we probably won't be able to get in touch with them."

"There's no cell signal down there either," one of the paramedics added.

"So how do you know if they're okay?" Lacy asked.

Archer shrugged. "All we can do up here is trust that God will take care of them."

Hannah did trust. She wanted to believe that God would protect them. But she also knew accidents could happen.

"Besides, Liam has extensive training in cave rescues," Archer continued. "There's no one better for this."

She believed him, but she couldn't help the nagging worry anyway.

The sky turned glorious shades of orange and pink, and then, as the sun sank below the horizon, shadows gathered in the dying light.

Hannah and Lacy talked about a trip Lacy and Neil were planning for January and about a new jigsaw puzzle Lacy had ordered for October's puzzle night. Lacy asked Hannah about how things were going at the restaurant. Finally, when it was fully dark and Hannah was starting to wonder if something had gone terribly wrong, there were noises from inside the cave. Voices echoed, growing louder as they neared the entrance. Everyone moved toward the opening.

Hannah saw the bright glow from the headlamps first, stark against the dark rock. A moment later, Liam's head and shoulders emerged from the hole, a huge smile on his face.

"We got them," he announced, heaving himself out of the cave entrance. "We got Chuck's things."

"Uncle Chuck is definitely not down there," Ryder added, emerging behind Liam. "But the things he left behind make it clear that everything we thought all this time was wrong."

"It definitely looks like your uncle did not die in that cave," Liam said to Hannah. "Judging by what we found, it really does seem as if he left his things there on purpose."

But no one had seen Uncle Chuck since the day of the accident—or supposed accident.

"So then, what *did* happen to him?" Hannah asked.

Ryder shook his head. "Your guess is as good as mine," he said. "All we know is that it's not what we thought."

Loved *Mysteries of Blackberry Valley?*
Check out some other Guideposts mystery series!

Whistle Stop Café Mysteries

Join best friends Debbie Albright and Janet Shaw as they step out in faith to open the Whistle Stop Café inside the historic train depot in Dennison, Ohio. During WWII, the depot's canteen workers offered doughnuts, sandwiches, and a heap of gratitude to thousands of soldiers on their way to war via troop-transport trains. Our sleuths soon find themselves on track to solve baffling mysteries—both past and present. Come along for the ride for stories of honor, duty to God and country, and of course fun, family, and friends!

Under the Apple Tree
As Time Goes By
We'll Meet Again
Till Then
I'll Be Seeing You
Fools Rush In
Let It Snow
Accentuate the Positive
For Sentimental Reasons

MYSTERIES OF BLACKBERRY VALLEY

That's My Baby
A String of Pearls
Somewhere Over the Rainbow
Down Forget-Me-Not Lane
Set the World on Fire
When You Wish Upon a Star
Rumors Are Flying
Here We Go Again
Stairway to the Stars
Winter Weather
Wait Till the Sun Shines
Now You're in My Arms
Sooner or Later
Apple Blossom Time
My Dreams Are Getting Better

Secrets from Grandma's Attic

Life is recorded not only in decades or years, but in events and memories that form the fabric of our being. Follow Tracy Doyle, Amy Allen, and Robin Davisson, the granddaughters of the recently deceased centenarian, Pearl Allen, as they explore the treasures found in the attic of Grandma Pearl's Victorian home, nestled near the banks of the Mississippi in Canton, Missouri. Not only do Pearl's descendants uncover a long-buried mystery at every attic exploration, they also discover their grandmother's legacy of deep, abiding faith, which has shaped and guided their family through the years. These uncovered Secrets from Grandma's Attic reveal stories of faith, redemption, and second chances that capture your heart long after you turn the last page.

History Lost and Found
The Art of Deception
Testament to a Patriot
Buttoned Up
Pearl of Great Price
Hidden Riches
Movers and Shakers
The Eye of the Cat
Refined by Fire

MYSTERIES OF BLACKBERRY VALLEY

The Prince and the Popper
Something Shady
Duel Threat
A Royal Tea
The Heart of a Hero
Fractured Beauty
A Shadowy Past
In Its Time
Nothing Gold Can Stay
The Cameo Clue
Veiled Intentions
Turn Back the Dial
A Marathon of Kindness
A Thief in the Night
Coming Home

A Note from the Editors

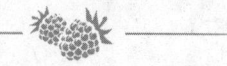

We hope you enjoyed another exciting volume in the Mysteries of Blackberry Valley series, published by Guideposts. For over seventy-five years, Guideposts, a nonprofit organization, has been driven by a vision of a world filled with hope. We aspire to be the voice of a trusted friend, a friend who makes you feel more hopeful and connected.

By making a purchase from Guideposts, you join our community in touching millions of lives, inspiring them to believe that all things are possible through faith, hope, and prayer. Your continued support allows us to provide uplifting resources to those in need. Whether through our communities, websites, apps, or publications, we inspire our audiences, bring them together, and comfort, uplift, entertain, and guide them. Visit us at guideposts.org to learn more.

We would love to hear from you. Write us at Guideposts, P.O. Box 5815, Harlan, Iowa 51593 or call us at (800) 932-2145. Did you love *A Likely Story*? Leave a review for this product on guideposts.org/shop. Your feedback helps others in our community find relevant products.

Find inspiration, find faith, find Guideposts.

Shop our best sellers and favorites at
guideposts.org/shop

Or scan the QR code to go directly to our Shop

More Great Mysteries Are Waiting For Readers Like *You*!

Whistle Stop Café Mysteries

"Memories of a lifetime....I loved reading this story. Could not put the book down...." —ROSE H.

Mystery and WWII historical fiction fans will love these intriguing novels where two close friends piece together clues to solve mysteries past and present. Set in the real town of Dennison, Ohio, at a historic train depot where many soldiers once set off for war, these stories are filled with faithful, relatable characters you'll love spending time with.

Mysteries & Wonders of the Bible

"I so enjoyed this book....What a great insight into the life of the women who wove the veil for the Temple." —SHIRLEYN J.

Have you ever wondered what it might have been like to live back in Bible times to experience miraculous Bible events firsthand? Then you'll LOVE the fascinating **Mysteries & Wonders of the Bible** novels! Each Scripture-inspired story whisks you back to the ancient Holy Land, where you'll accompany ordinary men and women in their search for the hidden truths behind some of the most pivotal moments in the Bible. Each volume includes insights from a respected biblical scholar to help you ponder the significance of each story to your own life.

Mysteries of Cobble Hill Farm

"Wonderful series. Great story. Spellbinding. Could not put it down once I started reading." —BONNIE C.

Escape to the charming English countryside with **Mysteries of Cobble Hill Farm**, a heartwarming series of faith-filled mysteries. Harriet Bailey relocates to Yorkshire, England, to take over her late grandfather's veterinary practice, hoping it's the fresh start she needs. As she builds a new life, Harriet uncovers modern mysteries and long-buried secrets in the village and among the rolling hills and castle ruins. Each book is an inspiring puzzle where God's gentlest messengers—the animals in her care—help Harriet save the day.

Learn More & Shop These Exciting Mysteries, Biblical Stories, & Other Uplifting Fiction at **guideposts.org/fiction**

MYSTERIES of BLACKBERRY VALLEY

Where There's Smoke
The Key Question
Seeds of Suspicion
A Likely Story

Bless those who persecute you; bless and do not curse. Rejoice with those who rejoice; mourn with those who mourn. Live in harmony with one another. Do not be proud, but be willing to associate with people of low position. Do not be conceited.

—Romans 12:14-16 (NIV)